THE ENEMY WITHIN

Stephen J. Schulhofer

The ENEMY WITHIN

Intelligence Gathering,
Law Enforcement,
and Civil Liberties
in the Wake of
September 11

A Century Foundation Report

The Century Foundation Press • **New York**

The Century Foundation sponsors and supervises timely analyses of economic policy, foreign affairs, and domestic political issues. Not-for-profit and nonpartisan, it was founded in 1919 and endowed by Edward A. Filene.

LIBRARY OF CONGRESS CATALOGING-IN-PUBLICATION DATA

Schulhofer, Stephen J.
  The enemy within : intelligence gathering, law enforcement, and civil liberties in the wake of September 11 / Stephen J. Schulhofer.
    p. cm.
"A Century Foundation report."
Includes bibliographical references and index.
  ISBN 0-87078-482-X
  1. Civil rights—United States. 2. National security—United States.
3. Terrorism—United States—Prevention. 4. Law enforcement—United States. I. Title.
  JC599.U5 S3855 2002
  363.3′2′0973—dc21

                                                          2002012687

FOREWORD

The implications of the shock waves from last September 11 are still not fully understood. Although it has become commonplace to talk about the many ways in which our lives have changed, we have a long way to go before we can be certain about the long- term effects on our society of the tragedy on that day. To be sure, there were earlier terrorist attacks on American soil, including the bombings of the World Trade Center in 1993 and the Oklahoma City federal office building in 1994. But these incidents caused scarcely a disturbance in the normal flow of everyday life for most citizens. Nor did they change the sense of personal safety most Americans long took for granted.

During the past twenty years, other assaults were launched against Americans abroad, including the bombings of U.S. embassies and military installations. But in large part, these events were treated as remote occurrences without direct implications for our way of life at home. So it is not surprising that, with the important exception of experts knowledgeable about terrorism, most Americans were convinced that high-casualty attacks were rare and distant, simply not something that could happen in the continental United States.

Shattering that complacency, September 11 jarred the nation into reactions that were all the more likely to be impulsive. Of course, significant changes in the government's agenda and in public attitudes were entirely justified. But with the first anniversary of the attacks at hand, the federal response has received remarkably little scrutiny. Few systematic efforts have been launched to weigh the benefits and costs of important legal and procedural changes since September 11, while some of the most far-reaching initiatives have gone largely unnoticed.

In this report, New York University law professor Stephen Schulhofer summarizes in detail the range of steps that has been taken to try to identify and apprehend potential terrorists living in the United States. As he catalogues the past year's transformations in law, policy, and management, Schulhofer raises hard questions that the nation until now has seemed unprepared to ask. Recognizing the public's legitimate desire to err "on the safe side" given the obvious severity of the threat, Schulhofer evaluates the changes from a pragmatic standpoint: Are they likely to be effective in combating terrorism? Would alternative approaches be preferable? Are adequate protections in place against abuse? Are the initiatives focused sufficiently on terrorism as opposed to more conventional crimes? Have fundamental constitutional protections been excessively compromised?

Although there is abundant room for debate about Schulhofer's conclusions, readers of this report are likely to come away from it convinced that policymakers ought to probe the questions he asks far more thoroughly than they have to this point. The system in place last September 10 evolved over the course of more than two centuries, formed gradually through the ebb and flow of politics, international conflicts, domestic crises, economic transformations, and other powerful forces. It is a system that sustained public support over those many decades through its transparency and accountability. Greater awareness of the many significant changes to that system since September 11, and more informed debate over their implications, will only strengthen it.

Nothing like the internment of Japanese-Americans during World War II has recurred during subsequent conflicts, largely because the American public ultimately recoiled at the extent to which that action violated the nation's fundamental principles. The far less sweeping post–September 11 detention of a large number of Muslim Americans, some of whom remain held without legal counsel or access to the media, has prompted muted unease. But the secrecy surrounding those detentions has deterred informed debate over the policy. The anniversary of September 11 seems an appropriate moment to begin a more open discussion about the trade-offs connected to the government's responses to date.

Thanks to the support of the John D. and Catherine T. MacArthur Foundation and the John S. and James L. Knight Foundation, The Century Foundation has been able to organize three working groups composed of bipartisan panels of scholars, experts, and former government officials. They are overseeing a number of studies and also may make their own recommendations abut some issues. In addition, we are publishing a number of studies addressing similar questions to those examined in this report, questions that have emerged over the past year. The topics explored include the pros and cons of instituting national identification cards, tracking visa holders more closely, and creating a North American security perimeter. The creation of a federal Department of Homeland Security, another important development on which we are focusing, involves a governmental change paralleled only by the reorganization of national security agencies to meet cold war demands in the years after World War II. The changes made fifty years ago, however, were built upon hard lessons learned during the conflict. Today, we must rely on our best guess about what will work because of the extraordinary circumstances in which we find ourselves.

We have a long way to go before the American response to a continuing threat of terrorism is completely thought out, let alone fully implemented. Along the way, we shall benefit greatly as a people by the research and reflections of knowledgeable scholars such as Stephen Schulhofer. On behalf of the Trustees of The Century Foundation, I thank him for this thoughtful and important contribution to our understanding.

RICHARD C. LEONE, *President*
The Century Foundation
August 2002

Contents

ACKNOWLEDGMENTS

The author wishes to acknowledge the excellent research assistance of New York University and University of Chicago law students Mendi Carroll, Bill Ferranti, Jennifer Huber, Angela Ramey, and Vanessa Stich.

Chapter 1

INTRODUCTION

An exponential increase in the resources and legal weapons devoted to counterterrorism efforts is a defining feature of our world since September 11. Budget dollars and the numbers of federal agents assigned to gathering intelligence have increased dramatically, and many new law enforcement initiatives have been put in place. For FBI surveillance and information storage operations alone, the latest federal budget provides an increase of nearly $200 million a year and more than two hundred new federal employees.[1] Congress has granted the executive branch sweeping new powers, most notably in the PATRIOT Act,[2] passed with little congressional debate, and virtually no dissent, on October 26, 2001, just six weeks after the attacks. And the executive branch has used rulemaking authority to assume many new powers on its own initiative, without congressional consideration or approval.

Few of us doubt that the threat of terrorism is real and that powerful law enforcement tools will be needed to contain it. At the same time, there can be no illusions about the impact of these new powers on liberty and privacy rights that most of us took for granted on September 10. The law enforcement measures recently put in place and additional initiatives still being developed unquestionably will curtail the liberty and privacy of both American citizens and foreign nationals within our borders.

Many Americans accept the entire package of new initiatives wholesale, perhaps without feeling any need to know much about the details of what national leaders judge necessary. This lack of close

1

scrutiny was understandable in the atmosphere of urgency and uncertainty that prevailed immediately after September 11. But we cannot afford to let it become permanent. Nothing could be more foreign to American democracy, or more dangerous, than the assumption that in a time of crisis, scrutiny and criticism of governmental action are unnecessary, unpatriotic, or obstructionist. No features of our political structure are more central and important than our commitments to separation of powers, checks and balances, and the maximum feasible degree of public discussion and debate—even in wartime.

With some distance from the shock of September 11, we are now in a position to begin assessing the steps taken, and their impact on important American freedoms. Indeed, with the war on terrorism likely to continue for years and probably decades to come, we cannot afford to suspend "for the duration" a careful evaluation of the many dramatic ways in which September 11 has altered the balance between security and liberty. We cannot afford to defer consideration of the need for these changes, their wisdom, and the dangers they may pose.

Much of this report is devoted simply to describing the new domestic intelligence-gathering and law enforcement efforts. Though this account is based on publicly available information, much of what is technically "available"—in the fine print of new statutes, regulations, and reports—is not at all widely known. An important first step in public understanding is simply to see the breadth and implications of the new measures being put in place.

The range of new initiatives is vast. Some, especially the new airport screening procedures, are well known and relatively well understood. Other new initiatives include lengthy detention of aliens lawfully in the United States who are not charged with any crime, complete secrecy concerning the identity and location of many of those detained, new powers to eavesdrop on attorney–client communications, and refusal to allow some of those held to communicate with an attorney at all. The recent initiatives also include new powers to conduct undercover infiltration and surveillance of political and religious groups, and increased wiretapping, electronic eavesdropping, and covert acquisition of Internet and e-mail communications, including increased powers to conduct these kinds of surveillance without probable cause or a judicial warrant.

On a different but equally important front, new laws expand government power to secretly obtain and review a customer's banking, brokerage, and other financial records—and any other business records—without the consent of the business or its customer, without any notice to the customer (before or after the event), and without even having any reason to suspect that the person targeted by the probe is involved in terrorism or any other any criminal activity. New laws also expand the obligation of banks and other financial institutions to track the transactions of their customers and to report "suspicious" customers to the government.

The new initiatives reflect the serious, extremely complex threats facing America. The specific justifications offered to support them deserve careful consideration, and they are discussed in detail in this report. Many of the measures, though unusual, reflect legitimate concerns and have been crafted with concern to protect liberty and privacy to the extent possible. Nonetheless, there are serious shortcomings in the federal response to September 11. Important individual freedoms have been sacrificed—often needlessly and unjustifiably.

Sifting through the broad array of counterterrorism initiatives and the many kinds of concerns they evoke, we can see three distinct and frequently recurring groups of problems. First, there are simply *bad compromises*—in several instances since September 11, valuable liberties have been eroded with little or no prospect of a useful law enforcement payoff. Second, there have been distressing instances of *September 11 opportunism*—investigative powers largely or totally unrelated to terrorism have slipped into the counterterrorism package and won approval without the careful scrutiny that proposals tied to a conventional law enforcement goal normally would face.

Finally, most important, and most persistently in the response to September 11, there are serious problems of *unchecked executive branch power*. Separate from what lawyers call "substantive" questions (Are there individual rights? How broad are governmental powers?) are questions of structure and procedure: How are the granted powers allocated? What controls will assure that officials, well-intentioned or otherwise, go no further than the substantive rules authorize them to go? In the American constitutional system, these crucial structural safeguards take three main forms: separation of legislative, executive, and judicial functions; checks and balances within and between the branches of government; and transparency—a sufficient degree of openness to permit informed public discussion and with it the additional checks and balances that press coverage and public scrutiny provide. Yet across a diverse spectrum of federal responses to

September 11, these structural safeguards are repeatedly, unnecessarily, and dangerously eroded; in some instances, traditional checks and balances have been entirely obliterated.

Whatever the need, post–September 11, to reposition the line between law enforcement power and individual rights, this perceived imperative does not in itself imply any need to suspend the mechanisms of accountability and control that traditionally frame governmental power. If anything, there may be *more* need, as government investigative power expands, for strong, effective checks and balances. Yet in the wake of September 11, the executive branch sought and obtained from Congress many new powers to act *unilaterally*, bypassing traditional forms of judicial review and control. And the executive branch has simply assumed many new powers on its own initiative, without congressional authorization or input. It has, again without congressional input, significantly reduced the role of the judicial branch and unilaterally overridden safeguards normally available to detainees and others under applicable state laws. Compounding concerns about the weakening of checks and balances, the executive branch has, again unilaterally, limited the ability of defense attorneys to assist those targeted for investigation, used new rules of secrecy to constrain oversight and criticism by the public and the press, and even reduced the internal supervision and control of investigators by their FBI superiors in field offices and at FBI headquarters. The executive branch arguments invoked to defend these measures are considered in detail, item-by-item, throughout this report. But the general pattern is important to notice, and it magnifies the concern that any of these measures individually should evoke.

There are seven more chapters in this report. First, though the present challenge to our security is unprecedented in character, it would be unrealistic to assess it in isolation. To provide some context, Chapter 2 briefly surveys previous national emergencies and the kinds of civil liberties limitations they prompted. Chapter 3 considers efforts to incarcerate and interrogate individuals suspected of terrorist links but not accused of any crime.* Chapter 4 reviews several steps recently taken to deny September 11 detainees unimpeded access to their

---

* This report does not address the presidential order authorizing the creation of military commissions to try aliens accused of terrorist activity. "Detention, Treatment, and Trial of Certain Non-Citizens in the War Against Terrorism," 66 Fed. Reg. 57,833 (Nov. 13, 2001). These commissions apparently were intended primarily for

lawyers. Chapter 5 considers the variety of ways in which government's powers of surveillance have expanded since September 11 through such tools as wiretapping, electronic surveillance, and monitoring those who use e-mail and the Internet. Chapter 6 examines new laws that enlarge government access to documents and files of financial, educational, and business records. Chapter 7 discusses recent Justice Department steps to give field agents greater freedom to build files and pursue investigations with reduced supervision by their FBI superiors. The final chapter identifies ten steps that deserve urgent attention in a balanced response to the challenges of September 11.

---

use in trying so-called unlawful combatants captured during military operations in Afghanistan or elsewhere abroad. At least as initially drafted, the order granted no jurisdiction over American citizens, and there was no attempt to invoke it to divest the civilian courts in the cases of either John Walker Lindh, an American captured in Afghanistan, or Zacarias Moussaoui, a French national who is the only alleged September 11 conspirator so far apprehended in the United States. The attempt to apply military jurisdiction to Abdullah al Muhajir, an American citizen arrested in Chicago, is discussed in Chapter 3.

Chapter 2

THE CONTEXT: RESTRICTIONS ON CIVIL LIBERTIES IN TIMES OF WAR

Throughout our history, the demands of national security have prompted wartime presidents to impose unusual limits on freedom of speech, the right to jury trial, and other individual liberties. Chief Justice Rehnquist wrote in a 1998 study of this history that "the government's authority to engage in conduct that infringes civil liberty is greatest in time of declared war."[1] World War II Attorney General Francis Biddle observed that wartime presidents often have paid little attention to constitutional niceties.[2] And Congress has often done likewise. There are many well-known examples.

During the Civil War, President Lincoln suspended the writ of habeas corpus and by proclamation made it a military offense, punishable by courts-martial (where the constitutional rights to jury trial and to independent, life-tenured judges would not apply), for anyone, civilians included, to obstruct military enlistment or engage in "any disloyal practice affording aid and comfort to rebels."[3] When America entered World War I, Congress made it a crime to express views that could hinder the war effort, and there followed numerous successful prosecutions for "sedition" and disloyal speech.

In World War II, President Roosevelt, with congressional approval, ordered the forcible relocation to internment camps of over 100,000 West Coast residents of Japanese descent, most of whom were native-born U.S. citizens. Martial law was imposed on Hawaii for the duration of the war. And when a turncoat enabled the FBI to

7

capture German naval officers who had landed in the United States, buried their uniforms, and begun efforts to sabotage war-related facilities, Roosevelt issued an order permitting their trial in secret before a military commission, which convicted them of spying and sentenced them to death. During the (undeclared) Korean War, President Truman seized the steel mills to forestall a labor dispute that would have interrupted production. During the (undeclared) Vietnam War, the Justice Department conducted "national security" wiretaps without judicial approval in cases involving "clear and present danger to the structure or existence of the Government," and it attempted to stop the *New York Times* and the *Washington Post* from publishing the so-called Pentagon Papers, a lengthy document stolen from Defense Department files that detailed the history of American involvement in Vietnam.

The Supreme Court has allowed wartime presidents a wide berth and often has hesitated to second-guess their actions. As Chief Justice Rehnquist's book notes, judges have been "reluctan[t] . . . to decide a case against the government on an issue of national security during a war."[4] But judicial deference to the president has not been uniform or unlimited. On the contrary, courts intervened and forcefully condemned many wartime presidential initiatives.

Ex Parte Milligan,[5] a striking Civil War example, presents important parallels to the military necessity arguments pressed today. Milligan, a citizen of Indiana, was arrested by the military commander in that district and charged with conspiring to "afford[.] aid and comfort to rebels."[6] On President Lincoln's orders, he was tried by a military commission and sentenced to death. Even though Indiana was threatened with invasion by Confederate troops at the time of the arrest, the Supreme Court rejected the president's position and held it unconstitutional to apply military law to civilians unless a rebellion or invasion "effectively closes the courts and deposes the civil administration."[7]

The issue was not technical. The Court noted that "it involves the very framework of the government and the fundamental principles of American liberty. . . . No graver question was ever considered by this court."[8] The justices curtly dismissed the argument the "laws and usages of war" could override the hallowed privilege of trial by jury[9] and treated as absurd the government's claim that Milligan could be deemed a "prisoner of war."[10] While acknowledging wartime security concerns, the decision gave them narrow scope: "If it was dangerous . . . to leave Milligan unrestrained of his liberty, . . . then present his case to the grand jury. . . , with proofs of guilt [and] try him according to the course of the common law. . . . Martial law cannot arise from a *threatened* invasion. The necessity must be actual and present . . . such as effectually closes the courts . . . . If martial law is continued after the courts are reinstated, it is a gross usurpation of power."[11]

In later decisions, the Supreme Court deferred to some wartime security claims but emphatically rejected others. The Court upheld prosecutions for sedition during World War I,[12] but First Amendment limitations advocated in the famous Holmes and Brandeis opinions in those cases were accepted eventually as setting the correct constitutional standard, and there were no formal efforts to criminalize criticism during subsequent wars.

During World War II, the Supreme Court upheld the use of a military commission to try the German saboteurs. But it stressed that this deviation from constitutional norms was limited to prisoners who acknowledged their membership in the enemy armed forces.[13] The Court upheld the legality of the initial order relocating citizens of Japanese descent,[14] a decision much criticized as overly deferential to the president, even in the uncertainty that prevailed immediately after Pearl Harbor. But the Court did not stand aside entirely. In 1944, nearly a year before the Pacific war ended, the Court ordered the release of detainees of Japanese ethnicity who were found to be loyal American citizens.[15]

Another World War II decision is especially pertinent to issues in the forefront today. In *Duncan v. Kahanamoku*, the Court held that, despite the state of martial law imposed in Hawaii, civilians could not be tried in military courts, even at a time (February 1942) when the islands still faced grave threats of further attack.[16] Duncan, a civilian, was charged with assaulting two Marine sentries at the Honolulu Navy Yard, with intent to hinder the discharge of their duty. Despite the obvious military security concern in that context, the Court reaffirmed the *Milligan* standard: civilians within U.S. territory who interfere with a military function must be turned over to civilian authorities unless the civil courts are no longer open and functioning.

Because Hawaii was in the theater of actual military operations and in ever-present danger of Japanese sabotage or invasion, two Justices stressed *in dissent* "the need for a zone of executive discretion within which courts must guard themselves with special care against judging past military action too closely."[17] But the Court's majority held instead that the paramount concern must be to restrain to the minimum any supplanting of the civilian judicial sytem: "[Our founders] were opposed to governments that placed in the hands of one man the power to make, interpret and enforce the laws. . . . Legislatures and courts are not merely cherished American institutions; they are indispensable to our government. Military tribunals have no such standing."[18] Concurring, Chief Justice Harlan Fiske Stone added, "The Executive has broad discretion in determining when the public emergency is such as to give rise to the necessity of martial law. [But] the military's judgment here is not conclusive that every action taken pursuant to the declaration of marital law was justified by the exigency. '[T]he allowable limits of military discretion, and whether or not they have been overstepped in a particular case, are judicial questions.'"[19]

Subsequent experience was similar; the courts *did* scrutinize and *did* overturn sensitive wartime decisions. In the midst of the Korean War, the Supreme Court held that President Truman's seizure of steel mills to maintain production of war materiel was unconstitutional.[20] During the Vietnam War, the Court *unanimously* rejected the Justice Department's claim of power to conduct national security wiretaps without judicial approval.[21] And the Court, acting at the height of the Vietnam War, refused the government's request to enjoin publication of the Pentagon Papers. Again, the Court declined to defer to executive branch claims for national security, even though the government had insisted that publication of this top-secret document would endanger our troops in the field and undermine ongoing military operations.[22]

The national security measures adopted since September 11 avoid many of the civil liberties restrictions imposed in earlier emergencies. In several respects, however, the September 11 initiatives compromise important freedoms in ways that previous presidents never attempted, even in the midst of formally declared wars. And important changes in the law have been adopted by the Department of Justice unilaterally, without public input or congressional approval. Open discussion of the wisdom and legality of new limitations on liberty, considered normal in previous wartime situations, is long overdue now.

Chapter 3

DETAINING SUSPECTED TERRORISTS

In the two months following September 11, approximately 1,200 foreign nationals living in the United States were arrested and detained by federal law enforcement agencies. Discussion of the precise numbers affected and the nature of their cases is hampered by the strict conditions of secrecy that continue to surround this program. It is known that of the 1,200 detainees, 718 initially were arrested on immigration charges; the remainder presumably were arrested on criminal charges, held as material witnesses, or perhaps held only on unspecified suspicions. By the end of November, about half remained in detention, including 93 named individuals charged with criminal offenses, 11 individuals held as material witnesses (with all records pertaining to them kept under seal), and 548 *unnamed* individuals held only on civil immigration charges. Nearly 40 percent of the detainees were Pakistani nationals, with most of the rest citizens of other Islamic countries. Of those held only on alleged immigration violations, 460 were still in detention, their identities undisclosed, on January 11, and it is believed that over 100 remain in custody at this writing (July 2002). Of the 460 still held in January, 380 were considered "active" cases; the remaining 80 individuals were in the "inactive" category, apparently no longer suspected of terrorist links; yet they were still in custody four months after September 11. Except for 93 individuals facing criminal charges, virtually none of the detainees has been identified publicly, and the locations where they are held also remain secret.[1]

The initial arrests based on immigration violations were not in themselves illegal. At this writing, it is believed that formal charges (for either immigration infractions or federal crimes) finally have been lodged against most September 11 detainees not already released. And those facing criminal charges have, with one important exception, received all procedural protections ordinarily available to American criminal defendants. (Extraordinary restrictions on communication with counsel are discussed separately in the next chapter.) The detentions nonetheless raise serious concern because of three unusual and possibly unconstitutional features—the strict conditions of *secrecy* that surround the program, the *length* of the detentions, and the absence of any *judicial review* at key stages.

UNPRECEDENTED SECRECY

The Sixth Amendment to the Constitution expressly grants criminal defendants the right to a public trial. Preliminary proceedings in criminal cases must be open as well, except when the court (after a *public* hearing) decides that extraordinary circumstances justify closure.[2] The administrative proceedings of the Immigration and Naturalization Service (INS) adhere to a similar standard. A toll-free phone number provides information on the status of pending cases, and hearings ordinarily are open to the public.

But these public-access principles have been suspended in the case of the September 11 detainees. On September 17, INS Chief Administrative Judge Michael Creppy, acting at the direction of Attorney General Ashcroft, issued a memorandum instructing immigration judges and administrators that all hearings involving September 11 detainees (designated as "special interest" cases by the Justice Department) must be closed to the public and that the cases must be specially coded in the INS database so that all inquiries, including calls to the INS toll-free number, will receive only the response that "information cannot be released regarding this case." Similarly, names and docket numbers for these cases must be deleted from court calendars posted outside courtrooms where immigration hearings are held.

Such secrecy not only hampers public awareness and assessment of INS actions but also poses a major burden for the detainees themselves.

Defendants in immigration proceedings have the right to be represented by counsel of their choice, but unlike the defendants in criminal
cases, they have no right to be provided counsel when they themselves
cannot obtain any. The onus is therefore entirely on the detainee to
find and retain counsel. But restrictions on the use of phones prevent
many detainees from contacting a lawyer, and the INS will not permit
lawyers and civil rights groups to contact the detainees unless the person seeking access already has the name of the potential client. [3] Even
after an attorney–client relationship is established, access in some cases
has been impeded by INS actions transferring detainees to different
locations without promptly notifying their lawyers.*

In October, two New Jersey newspapers brought suit, under the
New Jersey Freedom of Information Act, seeking disclosure of the
names of detainees being held by the INS in two of that state's county jails. When a New Jersey court ruled that state law required release
of the names, the Justice Department immediately adopted an administrative regulation overriding state law on this subject and required
state officials holding INS detainees to comply with INS secrecy regulations regardless of any state laws to the contrary. [4]

JUSTIFICATIONS FOR SECRECY

Litigation challenging the secrecy measures is now pending in several federal courts, and in its defense, the Justice Department has
offered four justifications. Secrecy, Attorney General Ashcroft has
argued, is necessary to protect the detainees themselves because "for us
to either advertise the fact of their detention or to provide the sugges-
tion that they are terrorists . . . would be prejudicial to their not only
privacy interest but personal interest." [5] More specifically, the department argues that naming the detainees could subject them to intimi-
dation and stigmatize those ultimately found to have no terrorist links;
the department also argues that releasing names of the detainees "may
deter them from cooperating"; "would reveal the direction and
progress of the investigation"; and "could allow terrorist organizations and others to interfere with the pending proceedings by creating
false or misleading evidence." [6]

---

*Other actions that restrict detainees' contacts with their lawyers are discussed in
Chapter 4.

The first justification is transparently inadequate. So far as we know, no one has suggested that suspected terrorists must be publicly identified as such; presumably the names of September 11 detainees should simply be released in a routine way along with the names of other INS detainees. In any event, many of the detainees *want* their names released so that they can more easily obtain help; the goal of protecting detainees cannot support a blanket policy of secrecy that includes cases in which the detainee himself prefers disclosure.

The other justifications are harder to dismiss outright. But all of them assume that detainees who are in fact terrorists will have associates at large, here or abroad, who somehow remain unaware that their confederate has been apprehended. This seems extremely unlikely. Detainees are allowed to make phone calls (on a restricted basis), and those contacted (counsel and family members) are legally free to reveal the detainee's identity. Indeed, if effective investigation depends on keeping a terrorist's cohorts ignorant of his detention, then any terrorist worth his salt will have defeated that goal from the first moment of his first call.

To be sure, there are occasional case-specific impediments to airing evidence in public. For such situations, courts have familiar, well-established procedures to ensure that national security is fully protected. The need for special treatment is itself a matter that can be explained to a judge, in a closed hearing if necessary, and approved by the court when circumstances truly warrant. It is perhaps not surprising that, in the only judicial decisions rendered on this problem to date, two federal courts have held the blanket secrecy measures unconstitutional, but the Justice Department continues to resist those rulings and seeks to overturn them.[7]

EXTENDED CONFINEMENT
WITHOUT JUDICIAL REVIEW

DETAINING FOREIGN NATIONALS

In a decision rendered less than three months before September 11, the Supreme Court made clear that aliens within U.S. borders, whether legally or illegally, must be afforded due process safeguards, including access to the courts and limits on the length of confinement.[8] Nonetheless, statutory and constitutional limits on detention never have been as strict in immigration proceedings as they are in criminal investigations.

In criminal cases, even where mass murder is concerned, the permissible duration of an investigative seizure (in the absence of probable cause) is measured not in days but in *minutes*, the outer limit normally being twenty minutes or in special circumstances perhaps an hour at most.[9] And even when supported by probable cause, a detention normally cannot exceed forty-eight hours prior to review of the probable cause allegation by a judicial officer.[10] Thereafter, a criminal defendant can be detained pending trial only if a court finds that no conditions of release can assure his appearance at trial or the safety of the community. This finding must be made after a formal hearing, in public, with right to counsel and a stringent burden of proof.[11] And the potential duration of post-arrest detention is inherently limited by the constitutional requirement that the accused be afforded a speedy trial.

Normal INS procedures roughly conform to these standards, though there is some added flexibility. Immigration officers can arrest aliens within U.S. borders without a warrant or probable cause, simply on the basis of suspicion that the alien has violated U.S. immigration laws. But prior to September 11, INS regulations required the agency to decide within twenty-four hours whether to release the detainee or file formal charges, which trigger a review process before an administrative judge.[12] All this changed for the "special interest" detainees arrested after September 11.

An "interim rule" adopted by the Justice Department on September 17, 2001, extended from twenty-four to forty-eight hours the ordinary time limit for filing INS charges. The new rule also provided that "in the event of an emergency or other extraordinary circumstance," the INS would be allowed "an additional reasonable period of time" to make its decision.[13] Moving in the same more flexible direction, the PATRIOT Act, passed on October 26, allows the INS seven days to decide whether to charge or release any alien certified as a "suspected terrorist."[14]

Though a seven-day delay would be unconstitutional in the case of a person arrested as a criminal suspect,[15] it is arguably a reasonable and permissible period in the case of immigration violators arrested as "suspected terrorists" in the unusual circumstances of September 11. But in numerous cases the INS has held September 11 detainees far

longer without filing charges. The PATRIOT Act makes as clear as
language can that seven days is the *maximum* time allowed: "The
Attorney General shall place an alien detained [as a suspected ter-
rorist] in removal proceedings, or shall charge the alien with a criminal offence, not later than 7 days after the commencement of such
detention. If the requirement of the preceding sentence is not satisfied,
the Attorney General shall release the alien."[16] Nonetheless, the INS
apparently takes the position that the PATRIOT Act's seven-day limit
does not supercede the "interim rule" adopted on September 17 and
therefore that it can take any "reasonable" time.[17] According to one
survey, 317 detainees were held more than forty-eight hours prior to
charge, 36 were held for more than twenty-eight days, and one
detainee was held for 119 days before being charged.[18]

Once formal immigration charges are filed, a foreign national
has the right to a hearing before an INS administrative judge (a semi-
independent official within the Department of Justice). The INS judge
decides whether the violation occurred and, if so, whether the alien
should be deported, allowed to leave voluntarily, or allowed to cure
the violation and remain. When deportation has been ordered, immigration statutes permit the INS to continue holding the alien for up to
90 days (180 days in exceptional circumstances), primarily to assure
that there is a foreign nation willing to receive him. The INS has
taken advantage of this authority to hold many of the September 11
detainees for long periods after deportation was ordered, pending
FBI "clearance." One survey reported that as of March 2002 many
detainees awaiting deportation "had spent more than 100 days in
jail, with no end in sight."[19]

In assessing these detentions, we should bear in mind that the
great majority of detainees ultimately were cleared of any terrorist
links and that many, when finally charged, were accused only of
minor immigration infractions such as overstaying a visa or working
illegally on a tourist visa. Two Pakistani men, for example, were each
detained for forty-nine days before being charged with overstaying
their visas.

Technical immigration violations of this sort normally result in
voluntary departure or prompt release pending regularization of the
immigrant's status. But the use of technical violations to support
deportation is not in itself the principal basis for concern. Aliens ordinarily have no right to remain in the United States, and general suspicions of hostile intent, far short of proof beyond a reasonable doubt,

can justify deporting them. In the September 11 cases, however, technical infractions are being used as a basis for keeping foreign nationals in custody to *prevent* them from leaving.

Holding such individuals for extended periods (in effect a form of preventive detention) is not always impermissible. But the problem here is that the executive branch has assumed power to decide *unilaterally* who will be detained and for how long.

Supreme Court decisions make clear that for preventive confinement to satisfy due process, measures like these must be strictly confined to limited time periods, with adequate safeguards against the arbitrary exercise of executive power. At a minimum, there must be provision for prompt *independent* review of relevant evidence in an adversary hearing, and the judge must find a substantial government need, reasonably related to the nature and duration of the detention.[20]

The September 11 detentions of foreign nationals are sharply at odds with these norms. Without statutory authority—and in apparent contradiction to the extended seven-day period that the PATRIOT Act allows for terrorism cases—the INS held some of these suspects for months without affording hearings and without charging any violation of criminal or administrative law. Even after review by semi-independent administrative judges, immigration rule violators who normally would be excused or deported were held—and are still being held—for preventive and investigative purposes, without any independent review of the grounds for suspicion or the relation of government need to the individual hardship created. Aside from the relocation of Japanese-Americans during World War II, the September 11 detentions appear to be unprecedented in terms of the unilateral, unreviewable executive branch powers on which they rest. And all of this has occurred under a far-reaching shroud of categorical secrecy. The effort to maintain the secrecy of these arrests and detentions may well be unparalleled in all of American history, World War II included.[21]

DETAINING AMERICAN CITIZENS

In several cases, small in number but important—indeed staggering—in their implications for civil liberty, the Justice and Defense Departments have invoked similar claims of unilateral executive power as a basis for detaining American citizens as well.

The first action of this sort was far removed from the setting of a typical criminal case. Yasser Esam Hamdi is an American citizen born to Saudi parents who at the time of his birth were living in Baton Rouge, Louisiana. Hamdi left the United States with his parents when he was less than a year old, and ever since he has lived in the Middle East. By his subsequent actions, he may have lost his American citizenship (the facts in that regard are disputed), but in any event he fought with al Qaeda and/or Taliban forces in Afghanistan, was captured in the fighting there, and was brought to Guantanamo Bay. When his American birth was discovered, he was transferred to a military brig in Virginia, and now he is being held under martial law pending trial by a military commission. The federal court in Alexandria, Virginia, appointed the federal defender there, Frank W. Dunham, Jr., to represent Hamdi, but the Defense Department blocked him from seeing Dunham, for alleged "national security" reasons.[22]

Though Hamdi's case has been in litigation for weeks, the courts have yet to rule on the government's claim of power to hold him for interrogation without access to counsel. The U.S. Court of Appeals twice has avoided a square decision on the matter, ruling first that Dunham did not have "standing" to raise the issue,[23] and then sending the case back to the district judge for further consideration of the government's national security arguments.[24] These delays, of course, prolong Hamdi's confinement incommunicado and in effect give the government what it seeks—more weeks of interrogation without interference from Hamdi's attorney. Many lawyers and civil liberties groups have expressed dismay about this case, but apparently little if any disapproval has been registered in the general public.

The next incident, much more troubling on its facts, involves a more conventional law enforcement situation. Abdullah al Muhajir (born Jose Padilla), an undisputed American citizen who was born in New York and subsequently converted to Islam, has lived most of his life in Chicago and Florida. He allegedly traveled to Pakistan to meet with al Qaeda operatives and allegedly discussed with them the possibility of building and setting off, somewhere in the United States, a bomb laced with radioactive material (a so-called dirty bomb). Acting on a tip, FBI agents arrested al Muhajir in Chicago in May and held him for a month as a "material witness." At the end of that period, when the government was due to produce him in court and lodge formal charges, the Justice Department chose not to do so.

Instead, Attorney General Ashcroft took some pride in announcing, in the midst of a visit to Moscow, that al Muhajir was being transferred to military custody and would be held indefinitely for questioning, with no right to see his lawyer and with no immediate prospect of being released, charged, or tried.

What the executive branch has asserted in the al Muhajir case is the unilateral power to imprison an American citizen and hold him incommunicado indefinitely, with no obligation to air its charges or present its evidence in a public hearing and with no judicial scrutiny of the basis for its actions. It is difficult to imagine a more significant departure from due process checks and balances that until now have always been taken for granted, even in wartime.[25] Yet again, there has been little expression of public concern.

JUSTIFICATIONS FOR DETENTION

The Justice Department's initial explanation for its moves in the al Muhajir case—that it did not have enough evidence to indict him— is extremely telling if true. But subsequently the government claimed instead that it chose to avoid indicting him because it needed more time to try to get information from him, a goal that supposedly would be thwarted if al Muhajir were granted normal rights to see his lawyer and to have a speedy trial. As a factual matter, this may (in part) be true. The government's tactic nonetheless seems poorly considered. Its actions will complicate, and perhaps render impossible, any effort to put al Muhajir on trial. But if trying him is not a priority, then allowing him access to a lawyer he can trust could be a more effective way to elicit his cooperation than isolating him against his will.

In any event, the government's goal, however worthy, does not warrant complete suspension of the rule of law. Though the government has characterized al Muhajir as an "unlawful combatant" subject to military jurisdiction, his status as an al Qaeda agent has yet to be admitted or demonstrated in any court.

No statute or administrative regulation authorized the Justice Department to transfer al Muhajir to military custody. It claims simply that its actions are "consistent with the laws and customs of war."[26] But the president's post–September 11 executive order establishing military commissions for the trial of "unlawful combatants" explicitly excludes U.S. citizens,[27] and even if it did not, the assertion of military jurisdiction under these circumstances seems impossible to square with constitutional limits applicable even in wartime. *Ex parte Milligan*,[28] which addressed conditions during the Civil War, and *Duncan v. Kahanamoku*,[29] which considered the security situation in Hawaii a mere two months after Pearl Harbor, both held that military law cannot be applied to civilians in American territory—even territory threatened with attack—if the civil courts are open and functioning, as they assuredly are in America now.

Only one historical precedent is in any way parallel to what the government has attempted in its treatment of al Muhajir. In World War II, eight German naval officers, all of them born in Germany, landed secretly on beaches in the United States, buried their uniforms, and proceeded to mix with the general population in preparation for sabotaging war-production facilities. President Roosevelt, by executive order, established a military commission to try them,[30] and in *Ex parte Quirin*,[31] the Supreme Court held this procedure constitutionally permissible under the circumstances.

One of the saboteurs, Haupt, claimed to have acquired American citizenship indirectly when his parents became naturalized citizens. But Haupt, like the others, had been living in Germany throughout the hostilities, and it was conceded that after Germany's declaration of war against the United States, he continued to serve on active duty in the German navy. In that situation, the Court found it irrelevant whether Haupt was technically an America citizen. On the undisputed facts, he was a combatant in the enemy armed forces. The military commission therefore had jurisdiction, under long-standing international law principles, to try him on charges that, if true, represented an unambiguous violation of the laws of war. As the Court stated, "We have no occasion now to define with meticulous care the ultimate boundaries of the jurisdiction of military tribunals to try persons according to the law of war. It is enough that petitioners here, upon the conceded facts, were plainly within those boundaries. . . . [They were] *admitted enemy invaders*."[32]

The government's attempt to detain al Muhajir indefinitely in a military brig is not remotely comparable. To begin only with the important legal formalities, it is critical to note the absence of a declaration of war, the absence of an executive order applicable to al Muhajir's case, and the apparent absence of any present plan to put him on trial in *any* court, civilian *or* military. But even putting aside these details, al Muhajir's situation is analogous to Haupt's only if he is an "admitted enemy invader"—that is, if he concedes that he gave allegiance to al Qaeda, joined one of its military brigades, and then surreptitiously entered the United States, out of uniform, in order to perform hostile acts behind our lines. But if such charges are disputed, as apparently they are, al Muhajir's position is in no essential way different from that of any other defendant facing legitimate allegations of serious misconduct.

A central premise of government under law is that executive branch officials, no matter how well respected, cannot by themselves have the power to imprison a citizen. No matter how serious the accusations they bring, they cannot expect to have those accusations accepted on faith. The truth of their accusations must be decided by independent judges, hearing counsel from both sides, in an adversarial trial.

Al Muhajir may be guilty of planning an extraordinarily serious crime. But it is the job of the courts to decide whether that accusation is true—even when the "unlawful combatant" charge amounts to an allegation of treason. Indeed, the Constitution makes explicit that treason charges call *not* for expedited military justice but for specially *heightened* safeguards: Trial must be held before a life-tenured federal judge, and "No person shall be convicted of Treason unless on the Testimony of two Witnesses to the same overt Act, or on Confession in open Court."[33] If the president, attorney general, and secretary of defense win public acceptance for their claim to exercise unilateral executive power in a matter of this sort, the damage to American democracy, founded on checks and balances, will be long-lasting and profound.

It is important to be clear about the nature of this problem. Despite the shock of September 11, there is nothing unprecedented about national security concerns in law enforcement. There is nothing unprecedented about the exigent demands of war, or the self-assurance of popular, well-meaning executive officials who believe they are being scrupulously fair and see judicial review as an unnecessary, time-consuming nuisance. We have been there before—many times. And now, as always in the past, national security concerns cannot justify granting the executive branch the power to suspend ordinary safeguards unilaterally. From the *Milligan* decision (1866) and the *Duncan* case (1946) through the steel seizure controversy (1952) and the rulings of the Vietnam era, the Supreme Court has been clear, consistent, and emphatic on this point.[34]

For similar reasons, the principal concern about these government actions does *not* center on the mere fact that suspected terrorists are being detained prior to conviction. There are circumstances in which preventive detention is justifiable, even essential. But when government can detain without filing charges and without revealing any information about the basis for what it has done, the executive branch has acquired power to deprive individuals of liberty and to incarcerate them under harsh conditions, with limited contact with counsel and the outside world, all without having to explain that action to the public or to any independent official. However much we respect the good intentions of the present attorney general and secretary of defense, such disregard for traditional checks and balances is a recipe for bad mistakes and serious abuses of power. When exercised in other countries, unchecked executive power of this sort—the unreviewable power to arrest, imprison, and hold incommunicado—is what we immediately recognize as a dangerous step in the direction of tyranny.

Chapter 4

RESTRICTING ACCESS
TO COUNSEL

One of the government's stated reasons for transferring al Muhajir to military detention was to prevent him from communicating with his lawyer. The Justice Department also has taken steps to restrict communication with counsel by detainees in the civilian justice system. On October 31, 2001, Attorney General Ashcroft promulgated an order authorizing federal jailers to monitor mail and conversations between any inmate and his lawyer when there is (in the attorney general's judgment) reason to suspect that the inmate will pass messages through the lawyer in order to further terrorist activity.[1] The order applies not only to convicted offenders but also to suspected terrorists awaiting trial and to detainees not charged with any crime or administrative infraction.

Previously, procedures to prevent inmate involvement in ongoing crime took two forms. A Bureau of Prisons regulation authorizes wardens to restrict or completely prohibit inmate contact and communication with outsiders (other than their attorneys) whenever those communications could result in serious injury to any individual. Inmates must be notified when such restrictions are put into effect, but judicial approval of the restrictions is not required.[2] Communications between an inmate and his attorney cannot be restricted, but they can be monitored surreptitiously, under court order, if a judge finds probable cause to believe that the attorney–client contacts maybe used to further criminal activity.[3] The new regulation

23

extends the first approach, so that attorneys, along with other visitors, can be monitored by administrative action, without judicial approval.

JUSTIFICATIONS FOR MONITORING CONTACTS WITH COUNSEL

The goal of the new monitoring program is to deter aid to terrorism and provide information about impending attacks, both surely legitimate objectives. And the attorney–client privilege does not extend to conversations used to further ongoing or future crime. But monitoring has an unavoidable impact on legitimate, constitutionally protected dimensions of the lawyer–client relationship. Inevitably, many innocent inmates will be monitored along with those actually involved in ongoing crime, and in both cases, government monitors inevitably will overhear discussion of matters that should remain confidential, including conversations about defense strategy or a defendant's statements explaining his role in the alleged offense. The mere possibility of such monitoring can inhibit the candid attorney–client communication that is essential for effective legal representation. As a result, courts traditionally hesitate to authorize monitoring of attorney–client communication, even in prison settings where the right to privacy is greatly diminished. Sixth Amendment (right-to-counsel) concerns may render such monitoring constitutionally suspect even in settings where Fourth Amendment (right-to-privacy) concerns do not apply.

Recognizing these Sixth Amendment issues, the new regulation requires that inmates and their attorneys be notified when the authority to monitor is being invoked, and all monitoring is conducted by a "privilege team" that is to have no contact with prosecutors and investigators involved in other matters concerning the inmate. When "firewall" safeguards of this kind are used to isolate monitors from other prosecutors, the Supreme Court has held that narrowly tailored eavesdropping need not inevitably violate the Sixth Amendment, at least if there is a legitimate law enforcement need for monitoring.[4] The Department of Justice argues that its new regulation complies with these standards, "carefully and conscientiously balances" the relevant interests, and "scrupulously protect[s]" the inmate's right to counsel.[5]

A closer look, however, suggests that the new regulation is in several respects unwise and possibly unconstitutional. There are three major problems. First, the regulation seems likely to impede the Justice Department's own goal of effective intelligence gathering, in ways that the department itself probably did not anticipate. Second, the regulation will in any case create a major impediment to effective attorney–client relationships. And finally, the harm to attorney–client relationships is unnecessary because other procedures, already in place, provide a way to achieve the department's antiterrorism objectives much more effectively and with much less harm to the right to counsel. We do not yet know the full extent to which the Justice Department will seek to invoke this new power, but the possibilities are alarming.

WILL MONITORING ACHIEVE ITS OBJECTIVES?

The twin goals of monitoring are to deter aid to terrorism and provide information about impending attacks. The program presumably will achieve its first goal without difficulty. Announced monitoring should deter most inmates who otherwise might use their attorney as a conduit to pass information. But it is unclear how monitoring will accomplish its second aim of providing access to useful intelligence. If anything, it seems likely to prove counterproductive in that regard.

Certainly, some detainees could have useful information about actual or suspected terrorist networks and operations. But they may not understand its value to the government or what they can gain for themselves by disclosing it. Government interrogators are trying hard to elicit that information, but inmates, unsure who they can trust, will likely hesitate to cooperate with their interrogators. Defense attorneys traditionally have served as essential intermediaries in alerting prosecutors that their clients have inside information and are willing to cooperate in return for assurances regarding the charge, the sentence, or the risk of deportation. Once warned that he is subject to monitoring, however, the inmate not only will be deterred from passing messages through his attorney to other terrorists but also will be deterred from telling the attorney anything else he knows about terrorist organization and plans. The attorney then will have no opportunity to advise his client whether to cooperate and reveal what he knows. As a result, the monitoring rule could well cause investigators to *lose* access to important information—information that could save lives, prevent further terrorist activity, and assist in identifying and apprehending important suspects.

WILL MONITORING VIOLATE SIXTH AMENDMENT RIGHTS?

Apart from its limited value and likely counterproductive effects, the monitoring order poses a significant obstacle to effective defense representation. And "privilege teams" insulated from other prosecutors cannot overcome the problem.

Establishing trust between lawyer and client is seldom easy, even in routine criminal cases, and especially so when counsel is court-appointed. In September 11 cases, these difficulties are compounded many times over by language barriers, by cultural differences, and by detainees' lack of familiarity with central features of our legal system, including the defense bar's tradition of commitment to the client and its independence from the government. When a detainee is told that government investigators will listen to all his discussions with his lawyer, attorney–client rapport and candid communication are bound to suffer. And aggravating these chilling effects on the lawyer–client relationship is the plausible fear that "privilege teams," despite their billing, may sometimes leak information.

Apart from the practical risk of leaks, no lawyer can tell his client that their legitimate discussions will remain confidential—even in theory. The Justice Department defends the new program as if it only would permit use of communications that assist ongoing acts of terrorism, and that may well be its intent. But once the government records an attorney–client conversation, after warning that it will do so, it will be free to use anything it learns against *other* individuals, including friends and relatives of the suspect. His family members, for example, could quickly find themselves in hot water if he mentions facts that put their immigration status in question. Other parties might have a right of access to the material under a variety of circumstances, and the government will be constitutionally *obligated* to disclose to other defendants anything it learns that could be considered exculpatory. Far from being in a position to reassure the client and encourage him to confide, a competent attorney will have to warn his client that much of what he says in *legitimate* attorney–client discussion could become known to others and could be used by the government. It is no exaggeration to conclude, as the American Bar Association does, that "the barriers to effective representation may become insurmountable."[6]

This interference with attorney–client communication is not only objectionable on its own terms; it also aggravates the practical drawbacks of monitoring from the government's own point of view. In cases affected by the new monitoring procedure, any criminal convictions obtained will be highly vulnerable to Sixth Amendment attack. (The validity of immigration proceedings, where there is a statutory right to counsel, may be affected as well.) Our ability to convict and punish individuals actually involved in September 11 or in planning similar terrorist attacks may be fatally compromised by this ill-considered power of surveillance.

ALTERNATIVES?

Monitoring has a legitimate goal (deterring aid to terrorism) that we cannot afford to neglect. But there is no need to incur its negative side effects (interference with the right to counsel) in order to remain vigilant. The regulation allows monitoring only when there are reasonable grounds to believe that attorney–client contacts may further terrorist activity. But whenever this is the case, the government can follow existing procedures and obtain a court order for *covert* monitoring, a procedure that is not only far more effective and far less likely to chill legitimate attorney–client discussion but is unquestionably legal as well. The only difference in the new approach, and undoubtedly its central motivation, is that it bypasses the courts. Yet the Justice Department rests its case entirely on the need to combat terrorism and says nothing about why it must bypass the courts in order to do so. By avoiding the normal requirement of a court order, the department in effect assumes unilateral power in an exceptionally sensitive area—eavesdropping on the work of opposing counsel.

It is hard to see how judicial involvement could pose any legitimate problem under the flexible statutory procedures already in place. A conventional wiretap order can be obtained by showing probable cause to believe that conversations will reveal evidence of ongoing or future crime. The required facts are for practical purposes identical to those needed to permit monitoring under the new regulation—

legally, "probable cause" simply means any "substantial basis."[7] Moreover, information is presented to the judge in a confidential proceeding, and the government need not identify its informants or other confidential sources.[8] The notions that judicial involvement will jeopardize the secrecy essential to gathering national security intelligence and that the subject matter is "too subtle and complex for judicial evaluation" were expressly rejected by the Supreme Court when it ruled in the *Keith* case (during the Vietnam War) that national security wiretaps are impermissible without a judicial warrant.[9]

The flexible probable-cause requirement applicable to conventional wiretaps is even further relaxed, moreover, when there is a basis to suspect that the target of the surveillance is the agent of a foreign power or an international terrorist group. In such situations, which by definition include all cases that qualify for attorney–client monitoring under the new rule, the government can conduct covert monitoring under a separate statute specifically designed for these sensitive situations.* Applications for these foreign intelligence warrants go to judges specially selected to afford extra assurance of expertise and confidentiality. Again, the government need not reveal the identity of its sources, and there is not even a need for probable cause to believe that conversations will reveal evidence of crime. The government need only show a substantial basis to believe that the target of surveillance is the agent of a foreign power or an international terrorist group, a showing that could scarcely be difficult for any inmate legitimately considered for this sort of monitoring in the first place.

The special foreign intelligence procedures were crafted by Congress with national security concerns specifically in mind, and they were revised in the PATRIOT Act in specific response to September 11. The ready availability of this statutory regime designed to deal with the subject removes any semblance of need for the Justice Department to address the problem by *unilaterally* assuming *unilateral* powers. Thus, the new regulations are ill-considered, largely counterproductive, and extremely harmful to the constitutional rights to counsel and due process. They also represent an inexplicable effort to bypass judicial checks and balances that Congress and the Supreme Court both consider workable and necessary to preserve.

---

*The operation of this statute, the Foreign Intelligence Surveillance Act (FISA), is discussed in Chapter 5.

Chapter 5

ENHANCING SURVEILLANCE POWERS

A major Justice Department goal in the aftermath of September 11 has been to expand its ability to gather intelligence on terrorist activity through physical searches, wiretapping, electronic surveillance, and newer, more sophisticated means. Working under enormous pressure and time constraints, the Justice Department, in a matter of days, assembled a package of several dozen proposals to amend existing statutes to that end. Congress, likewise acting quickly, approved the proposals with minimal hearings, little change, and none of the customary congressional committee reports.

Though the amended statutes are daunting in their detail and technical complexity, there should be no mistaking their concrete impact on the daily lives and privacy of ordinary, law-abiding people. Yet there has been little informed public discussion of the nature and wisdom of these changes. Many (probably most) Americans feel that law-abiding citizens have nothing to hide and should welcome rather than fear this enhancement of government surveillance powers. They argue that reductions in our privacy, no matter how extensive, are amply justified by the obvious need to do what we can to prevent further, possibly even more catastrophic, terrorist attacks. Others (a relatively small minority) argue that sacrificing basic privacy rights will simply make us less free without making us more secure and will amount to destroying our freedom in order to defend it.

Neither of these positions captures the complex reality of the expanded surveillance powers. Many of the new provisions simply correct oversights in prior law, eliminate pointless administrative obstacles, or adjust statutory language to new technologies. For example, prior law allowed courts to authorize "roving" surveillance (a surveillance not tied to a particular telephone) for domestic law enforcement purposes, but there was no parallel basis for courts to authorize roving surveillance in foreign intelligence investigations, a domain where government normally has more latitude. Similarly, through a quirk in statutory wording, government could use a search warrant to obtain records of unopened e-mail but not records of unopened oral messages in a voice-mail system. The law permitted the use of subpoenas and search warrants to obtain communication records from telephone and Internet-access companies, but it required a more cumbersome procedure, with notice to the customer and a full adversary hearing, to obtain the same information from cable companies, many of which now provide identical telephone and Internet services. And pre–September 11 law, by denying federal judges the power to issue search warrants with nationwide effect, required prosecutors to file a separate search warrant application in each federal district where surveillance might occur. The PATRIOT Act corrects these anomalies.[1] Though these changes obviously confer surveillance powers that did not exist before, they should not be the least bit controversial.

At the opposite extreme, many provisions short-circuit routine checks and balances, expand government access to private information of little intelligence value, and enlarge powers to investigate offenses entirely unrelated to terrorism. These provisions have likewise drawn little attention or criticism, and it is not hard to see why law enforcement officials would find them attractive. But even from the perspective of those who would willingly sacrifice their privacy in return for added protection against terrorism, provisions that enhance government power to investigate run-of-the-mill state and federal crime seem very difficult to justify as wartime emergency measures.

Many of the other new provisions provide potentially useful surveillance capabilities but at a significant cost to personal liberty. Especially important changes affect the privacy of e-mail, Internet browsing, banking and brokerage records, the educational records of every student, and the personnel files of every employee. In these instances, there is a plausible case for granting new powers in response to a new threat, but as yet there has been little accurate recognition of the price paid and little reasoned debate about whether the supposed benefits are likely to be worth their cost. Enacted in an atmosphere of urgency that made careful assessment all but impossible, some of these provisions involve potentially alarming departures from traditional limits on executive branch investigative power. Several are possibly or probably unconstitutional. Others, even if constitutional, dilute or obliterate important statutory safeguards.*

Measures in this third group, where there are both real benefits and real costs, receive a close look in the discussion that follows. The chapter examines first the general need for new surveillance tools, a concern across the entire spectrum of new measures. It then considers the issues raised by specific new powers to conduct electronic surveillance and physical searches without meeting traditional prerequisites. The next chapter examines related issues posed by new powers to gain access to documents and records in previously private financial, educational, and business files.

THE NEED FOR NEW SURVEILLANCE POWERS

In the first weeks after September 11, it was widely assumed that our intelligence agencies had been denied the use of investigative tools that could have provided warning of terrorist plans. The proposals eventually embodied in the PATRIOT Act reflect that assumption. They draw attention, over and over, to areas where the Justice Department had been denied various sorts of investigative power. That emphasis, whatever its purpose, had the effect of deflecting attention from questions about what the department could have done—or had done—within its existing powers; it implied instead that legal restrictions and civil liberties were in substantial measure to blame for the intelligence failures leading up to September 11.

That conclusion may turn out to be accurate, but many details now emerging suggest a more complicated story. The information remains fragmentary because President Bush has yet to call for the kind of comprehensive independent inquiry that President Roosevelt

---

* The PATRIOT Act includes a "sunset" provision, so that certain new powers will lapse if not re-enacted by the end of 2005, but many of the most significant statutory changes are exempted from this proviso and will remain in effect indefinitely. (See PATRIOT Act §224.)

ordered immediately after Pearl Harbor. Absent such an inquiry, the view attributing primary significance to legal restrictions remains only one of several possibilities. And from what we now know, that explanation no longer seems the most likely. Yet we urgently need to understand whether the measures being put in place are correcting or completely overlooking our weaknesses. However unpleasant and sensitive this inquiry may be, a continued unwillingness to pursue it will be dangerous to our security.

For example, a detailed FBI assessment of its counterterrorism capabilities, the "Director's Report on Terrorism" completed in spring 2001, found numerous weaknesses and made extensive recommendations, but they focused not on legal restrictions but rather on short-falls in available personnel, organization, computer quality, and analytic capabilities.[2] The report stressed above all that an effective counterterrorism effort required more budgetary support. Yet on September 10, in a political environment that then gave high priority to shrinking "big government," Attorney General Ashcroft rejected an FBI request for an additional $58 million to fund a strengthening of its counterterrorism effort.[3]

Moreover, government agents *had* picked up many clues, some of which were reasonably revealing. The primary problem on September 11 therefore may not have been the legal obstacles to surveillance or even a failure to pick up the telltale facts, but rather our inability to understand the information we had. As one FBI agent recently put it, "We didn't know what we knew."[4] If what we lack is not raw data to analyze but the ability to separate significant intelligence from "noise," then augmenting the volume of information flowing into FBI files will not help and may even aggravate the difficulty. Recent efforts to enhance staffing, computer functions, and analytic capability[5] will mitigate this problem, but not if they are counterbalanced by equivalent growth in the volume of raw data collected. Before September 11, the Treasury Department had recognized that an excessive influx of financial intelligence reports was *interfering* with its law enforcement capabilities.[6] Yet the steps taken since September 11 pay little heed to this side of the intelligence-gathering equation.

There also are disturbing indications that the FBI failed to make effective use of legal tools it already had at its disposal. On May 24, 2002, in response to a freedom-of-information lawsuit primarily concerned with another matter, the FBI released a confidential memorandum that to date has received little public attention. The memorandum, sent to an FBI associate general counsel in April 2000, reveals that an official in the Justice Department's Office of Intelligence Policy and Review was voicing intense concern about mistakes being made at the FBI's International Terrorism Operations Section (ITOS), and in particular by that Section's UBL (Osama Bin Laden) Unit.[7]

Referring to this Justice Department official, the memo reports, "To state that she is unhappy with ITOS and the UBL Unit would be an understatement of incredible proportions." The memo refers to a number of recent FBI errors in counterterrorism surveillance and concludes that "you have a pattern of occurrences [indicating] an inability on the part of the FBI to manage its FISAs [foreign intelligence surveillance operations]." A later episode, now well publicized, in which a supervisor prevented Minneapolis agents from obtaining a warrant to search Zacarias Moussaoui's computer, just a month before September 11, apparently was not an isolated incident. It appears that a pattern of missteps continued for many critical months when existing tools, properly used, might have made a difference.

It is important to be precise about this criticism: No one yet knows exactly how important such problems were or how they fit into the larger picture. What seems certain is that not making a comprehensive effort to find out is inexcusable. Conferring additional powers could be useless until these kinds of problems are corrected—and unnecessary afterward. Meanwhile, a preoccupation with dismantling civil liberties "obstacles" will divert energy and attention from problems that may matter much more. The notion that has largely prevailed since September 11—that we should grant federal investigators any tool that might bring to light any telltale clue—is dangerously simplistic.

THE NEW SURVEILLANCE TOOLS

Against the background of these general uncertainties about the need for additional federal surveillance powers, four new developments warrant detailed discussion:

- new authority to monitor the source and destination of e-mail and Internet activity ("pen register" and "trap and trace");

- enhanced capability for surveillance of e-mail content ("Carnivore");

- increased authority to conduct clandestine physical searches; and

- enhanced opportunities to classify surveillance as a foreign intelligence operation not subject to normal Fourth Amendment safeguards.

Before discussing developments in these areas, however, it will be useful to consider first the constitutional and statutory framework in which they have occurred.

Constitutional and Statutory Principles

The Fourth Amendment

The foundation for protecting privacy and limiting government's power to intrude is the Fourth Amendment's prohibition of "unreasonable searches and seizures." Subject to a few narrowly drawn exceptions, the Fourth Amendment permits an investigative search only when it is supported by probable cause and a warrant. That is, investigators must have "a substantial basis" to believe that a search will reveal evidence of criminal activity, and a neutral judicial officer, concurring in that assessment, must authorize the search in a court order that "particularly describ[es] the place to be searched, and the persons or things to be seized."[8]

Several ideas are central to this constitutional regime. One, often misunderstood, is that those who are in fact engaged in criminal activity have no claim to be shielded from governmental intrusion; once probable cause exists, their houses, papers, and effects are fair game for any search that could yield evidence of past or ongoing offenses. The point of the probable cause requirement, therefore, is not to shield those who "have something to hide" but rather to ensure that searches *will* focus on individuals who are likely offenders and will not subject innocent, law-abiding citizens to disruptive, frightening, intrusive search and surveillance practices.

The second central idea concerns checks and balances. Hard experience made clear to the Constitution's Framers that without some outside control, investigators in the executive branch, even when acting in good faith, too quickly find "probable cause" and too easily abuse their power to search. The Fourth Amendment therefore requires that the judgment about probable cause ordinarily be made by a neutral judicial officer who will narrowly define the permissible scope of a search before it occurs.

It is obvious, but in the present environment probably necessary to stress, that the requirement of independent judicial approval does not imply doubt about the good intentions of a particular generation of FBI agents. To enforce the warrant requirement, as a unanimous Supreme Court did in the *Keith* case at the height of the Vietnam War, does not reflect any lack of respect for the administration then in power or its attorney general. As most attorneys general have themselves understood, checks and balances—and the warrant requirement in particular—simply reflect the consistent verdict of history, from the eighteenth century onward, that grave abuses are all too likely if investigators—even conscientious, well-trained investigators—are permitted to search without judicial approval. In the *Keith* case, the Court acknowledged that "[t]here is, no doubt, pragmatic force to the Government's position"[9] concerning the risks of the warrant procedure in national security cases. Nonetheless, the Court held that compliance with the traditional warrant requirement remained essential. Justice Powell wrote for the Court:

> History abundantly documents the tendency of Government—however benevolent and benign its motives—to view with suspicion those who most fervently dispute its policies. Fourth Amendment protections become the more necessary when the targets of official surveillance may be those suspected of unorthodoxy in their political beliefs.[10]

The third central idea qualifies the first two because it limits Fourth Amendment safeguards to the domain of "searches" and "seizures," not other types of investigative work. A government intrusion is considered a "search" only if it invades a "reasonable expectation of privacy."[11] Use of a wiretap or hidden microphone is a search, for example, but the Supreme Court has held that an undercover agent who listens to conversations in his presence is not engaged in a search (even if he records and transmits what he hears), because others in the room know he is there and assume the risk that he may not keep their confidences.[12]

By similar reasoning, the Supreme Court has held that many records habitually considered "private" are not protected by the Fourth Amendment. Government inspection of a bank customer's records is not a search, the Court reasoned, because the customer made the records available to the bank and assumed the risk that a bank employee would see whatever information they contain.[13] And installing a device that secretly records the telephone numbers dialed from a suspect's phone (a so-called pen register) is not a search (though listening to the calls would be), because, the Court said, the suspect "voluntarily conveys those numbers to the telephone company when he uses the telephone," and he "has no legitimate expectation of privacy in information he voluntarily turns over to third parties."[14]

STATUTES AND REGULATIONS

Although the Constitution does not require probable cause or a warrant for surveillance methods not considered a "search," many people consider the information these techniques can reveal to be personal and sensitive. For that reason, and because these techniques are easily misused, other legal restrictions have been adopted. Administrative regulations limit the Justice Department's use of undercover informants. Congress has enacted statutory procedures to limit the use of pen registers, access to customer financial records, and access to student educational files. Two statutory systems are especially important for understanding the significance of the new laws enacted after September 11—Title III and FISA.

TITLE III. Wiretapping and electronic surveillance pose special problems at both the constitutional and statutory levels. Because there *is* a reasonable expectation of privacy in the content of personal communication in most non-public settings, these communications can be monitored only on the authority of probable cause and a warrant. But the Fourth Amendment prohibits "general" searches (so-called fishing expeditions) and expressly specifies that a valid warrant must "particularly describ[e] the place to be searched, and the persons or things to be seized."[15] A warrant authorizing investigators to record or scan all conversations on a certain phone would violate this particularity requirement, and in 1967, the Supreme Court held unconstitutional a New York statute providing for a judicially issued surveillance warrant that was a "broadside authorization" of this sort.[16]

Congress responded the next year by creating a detailed regime to limit the scope of such surveillance and to enable eavesdropping and wiretapping warrants to meet Fourth Amendment particularity requirements. The statute (commonly known as Title III) permits surveillance only for enumerated, especially serious crimes, limits the time period of surveillance, requires a specific showing of need to obtain extensions of this time, requires efforts to minimize eavesdropping on innocent parties, mandates prompt reports to the court of the surveillance results, and regulates the manner in which the results can be used. [17]

Title III specified, however, that none of its requirements would "limit the constitutional power of the President to take such measures as he deems necessary to protect the United States against [any] clear and present danger to the structure or existence of the Government."[18] This provision seemed to imply that "national security" wiretaps in both domestic and foreign investigations could continue outside the restrictions of Title III, and successive attorneys general had consistently asserted such a power since at least 1946. But in 1972 (during the Vietnam War), the *Keith* case held that the president had no such constitutional power in the case of domestic individuals and organizations having "no significant connection" with a foreign power. As a result, the Court ruled, surveillance of such *domestic* targets—even in "clear and present danger" situations—is unconstitutional in the absence of a judicial warrant that meets Fourth Amendment particularity requirements (such as those detailed in Title III).[19] But the Court left open the possibility of broader presidential authority in the case of surveillance of foreign powers and their agents.

FISA. To formalize a broader foreign intelligence power, Congress enacted the Foreign Intelligence Surveillance Act (FISA) in 1978.[20] As with surveillance under Title III, FISA surveillance can target U.S. citizens as well as foreign governments and foreign nationals. As with Title III, FISA normally prohibits surveillance in the absence of a judicial warrant and imposes time limits and minimization procedures. But FISA provides greatly simplified procedures for obtaining and executing foreign intelligence warrants, and these simplified procedures apply to physical searches as well as electronic surveillance. Applications for a FISA warrant go to specially selected federal judges, FISA imposes minimal judicial control over the particularity and scope of the search, and most important, there is no need for probable cause to believe that the surveillance or physical search will reveal evidence of crime. Thus, although FISA requires a court order, the judge's role is far more limited than in domestic law enforcement situations, and the conventional probable cause requirement is eliminated entirely.

There are two significant prerequisites for FISA surveillance without traditional probable cause. The government must show probable cause (that is, some substantial basis) for believing that the surveillance target, whether an American or foreign national, is the agent of a foreign power or a member of an international terrorist group. And, as FISA stood prior to September 11, the government was required to certify that "the purpose of the surveillance is to obtain foreign intelligence information."[21] The premise of FISA is that foreign intelligence surveillance is justified without traditional probable cause, because its aim is not to gather evidence for criminal prosecution but to counter the clandestine intelligence activities of foreign nations and to protect the United States from attack by hostile foreign powers. The courts have uniformly upheld the constitutionality of FISA surveillance, even in the absence of traditional probable cause, because "governmental interests in gathering foreign intelligence are of paramount importance to national security, and may differ substantially from those presented in the normal criminal investigation."[22]

SURVEILLANCE DEVELOPMENTS AFTER SEPTEMBER 11

The pre–September 11 regime of constitutional and statutory limits on surveillance and intelligence gathering was a complex mixture of stringent restraints, permissive powers, and awkward compromises. The PATRIOT Act shifted this balance in the direction of greatly expanded investigative power, especially by increasing opportunities to use e-mail and Internet searches, to conduct clandestine physical searches, to search under flexible FISA standards, and to use all these new opportunities to investigate crimes entirely unrelated to terrorism.

Monitoring the Source and Destination of E-mail and Internet Activity ("Pen Register" and "Trap and Trace")

Pen registers record telephone numbers dialed from a suspect's phone, and trap-and-trace devices record the numbers from which incoming calls originate. Pre–September 11 law prohibits use of these devices without a court order, but the order can be obtained without a showing of probable cause; the investigator must simply certify to the court "that the information likely to be obtained . . . is relevant to an ongoing criminal investigation."[23] Pen-register and trap-and-trace orders are permitted even when the target is not a suspect in the investigation, and unlike surveillance and searches under a traditional warrant, the investigator is not required to report to the court on the results obtained. The lesser safeguards are justified on the premise that these devices record only non-private information and do not reveal the content of calls or even the identity of the participants.

The PATRIOT Act extends the definition of pen-register and trap-and-trace information, previously restricted to telephone numbers, to include analogous origin and destination identifiers for e-mail and Internet browsing, specifically "routing, addressing, and signaling information."[24] The change is significant because routing information for e-mail and web transmissions can reveal much more about subject matter and the identity of participants than a mere telephone number does. The identity of a website, for example, can be as content-specific as the titles of books borrowed from a library or movies rented from a video store. Although the new definition specifically excludes "the contents of any communication" (presumably the subject line and body of a message), it implies that pen-register and trap-and-trace powers do reach user identification and subject-matter information embedded in the e-mail and Internet routing details.

The result of this expanded definition is that federal and state investigators can now access such information without probable cause, without any obligation to report their results to a court, and even when the person monitored is not in any way a suspect. The only requirement is that the information to be obtained may (in the investigator's judgment) be "relevant to an ongoing criminal investigation."

This new Internet surveillance power presumably can provide a useful tool in antiterrorism investigations. Even so, there would be little lost—and much gained for the privacy of millions of law-abiding Internet users—if this sort of monitoring required probable cause, or at least a showing of objective grounds to consider the target a potential suspect. But regardless of how one might choose to resolve this issue, the expanded powers are troubling and hard to defend because they are not limited to terrorism investigations. The PATRIOT Act grants expanded pen-register and trap-and-trace powers for use in federal and state investigations concerning *any* crime. Moreover, despite the uncertainties surrounding this technology and its capacity to reveal subject-matter detail, the pen-register and trap-and-trace amendments were exempted from the PATRIOT Act's sunset provision, and accordingly, they will remain in effect indefinitely, with no obligatory congressional reassessment.

Fair-minded people no doubt can disagree about the relative costs and benefits of expanded Internet monitoring, and some of the necessary facts simply are not yet available. What seems clear and undeniable, however, is that expanded law enforcement power to investigate *any* federal or state crime cannot be considered an antiterrorism measure. There is quite simply no justification for including this power in emergency legislation passed with great deference to an unusual law enforcement need.

Surveillance of E-mail Content ("Carnivore")

Carnivore is a pre–September 11 software program developed by the FBI, which recently gave it the new and less ominous name DCS 1000. Carnivore enables the FBI to enter the system of an Internet service provider (ISP), such as AmericaOnline, and record information passing through the ISP's network. It thus allows the FBI to monitor Internet and e-mail transmissions, including their content. In principle, Carnivore should be programmed to operate selectively, capturing only information that satisfies pre-set requirements. Thus, Carnivore can be used as a pen-register or trap-and-trace device, and it can also be used to focus on selected content, a search that is potentially better targeted and less intrusive than a traditional wiretap.

Only one provision of the PATRIOT Act addresses Carnivore. It requires that when a law enforcement agency uses its own software system, such as Carnivore, as a pen-register or trap-and-trace device, the agency must keep and provide to the court a record of the information collected, the officers involved in collecting it, and the date and times when the software was used. The act in effect legitimates the use of Carnivore without probable cause, despite its ability to capture and record content, provided that it is configured to record only origin and destination identifiers. But, reflecting concerns about Carnivore's potential for overbroad sweeps and other misuse, the act imposes safeguards not required for conventional, less powerful pen-register and trap-and-trace technologies.

The use of Carnivore to capture the *content* of e-mail and Internet traffic is a search governed by the usual legal restrictions (Title III and FISA). The post–September 11 legislation confers no new authority for Carnivore searches, other than the expanded powers it confers for surveillance methods generally. But Carnivore searches will undoubtedly become increasingly important as antiterrorism efforts and Internet usage expand.

Carnivore's potential for voraciously and indiscriminately devouring e-mail content make it a potentially serious threat to the privacy of on-line communication. The Carnivore software may fail to filter out unrelated content, and even if its filters work properly, agents who have access to it may deliberately or inadvertently misuse it. Finally and perhaps of greatest concern is the "back-door" problem. ISPs currently take great care to maintain the security of their networks, but Carnivore is designed to bypass all ISP security systems. This capability opens up a back door into the ISP's network, which could be exploited not only by a rogue agent but by any outsider able to hack into the FBI's Carnivore computers. An unauthorized user could spy on particular individuals or obtain their bank and credit-card information without being detected by the ISP's security system.

An Illinois Institute of Technology (IIT) study team, in an independent technical review commissioned by the Department of Justice, concluded in a December 2000 report that many of the worst fears concerning Carnivore are unfounded.[25] The IIT report found that Carnivore is a one-way system that can only receive and record; it cannot alter information in the network, block network traffic, or shut down a website. Moreover, Carnivore, according to the IIT report, can function only when its filter is highly selective; it does not have enough power (at present) to spy on everyone or to record all e-mails flowing through an ISP network.

Nonetheless, Carnivore filters can malfunction. Although the IIT report found that properly configured Carnivore filters will work as intended, serious failures have occurred. In one of the worst, FBI agents conducting an e-mail surveillance of an al Qaeda target discovered in March 2000 that Carnivore had recorded not only the target's e-mail but that of many other network users. An FBI memo of April 5, 2000, reported that "[t]he FBI technical person was apparently so upset that he destroyed all the e-mail take."[26]

The IIT study, moreover, reported other "significant deficiencies" in the Carnivore system. When used for pen-register and trap-and-trace purposes, it sometimes recorded more detail than authorized. It could be configured to perform broad sweeps far exceeding the permissible scope of a court-ordered search. FBI protocols did not sufficiently protect access to recorded information and physical access to Carnivore computers. Most important, the system's structure made it impossible to identify the individual agents using Carnivore, so that supervisors could not determine which agent did what in connection with its operation. As a result, the study team "did not find adequate provisions (for example, audit trails) for establishing individual accountability for actions taken during use of Carnivore."[27] To date (more than eighteen months after the IIT report was completed), the FBI has given no indication that these deficiencies have been addressed. Until they are, Carnivore will continue to pose a troubling and probably increasing threat to the privacy of Internet communication.

CLANDESTINE PHYSICAL SEARCHES

An important Fourth Amendment safeguard is the requirement of immediate notification when a search is conducted. Officers executing a warrant must knock and announce their presence before entering, except when doing so would expose them to danger or risk destruction of the evidence sought.[28] Similarly, the officers must give a copy of the warrant to the occupant or leave it at the premises if she is not present, again subject to a narrow exception for situations where such notice would endanger lives or seriously impede an investigation. These notice provisions serve to ensure that the target of the search will know that it occurred and have an opportunity to ensure that the particularity limitations of the warrant were respected.

Until September 11, exceptions to these notice requirements were governed by judicial decisions that examined on a case-by-case basis the need for conducting a clandestine search (a so-called sneak and peek) without immediate notification. The PATRIOT Act adds to federal law a provision that for the first time gives statutory authorization for clandestine intrusions and defines in broad terms the grounds that can justify delay in notifying the target that her home was searched.[29]

A reasonable argument can be made that the case law on clandestine searches needed to be clarified by legislation. A reasonable argument can likewise be made that the broad sneak-and-peek authority codified in the PATRIOT Act is preferable to the more restrictive view endorsed in some of the cases. Arguments can fairly be made in the other direction as well. But however that debate might best be resolved, this problem has nothing to do with the fight against terrorism. For international terrorism cases, authority to conduct clandestine searches already existed—in much broader terms—under FISA.[30] The new authority conferred by the PATRIOT Act is simply not needed for such cases, nor is it limited to terrorism cases; it is available in *any* criminal investigation. And because the new sneak-and-peek authority is exempted from the PATRIOT Act's sunset provision, it will remain in effect indefinitely. There was no justification for adding this issue to an already large emergency agenda after September 11 and for using the momentum of that occasion to obtain endorsement for the Justice Department's preferred approach to an unrelated problem.

FOREIGN INTELLIGENCE SURVEILLANCE WITH DILUTED SAFEGUARDS

Surveillance under FISA has always been permitted for longer periods than conventional Title III surveillance, and the PATRIOT

Act provides even more flexibility in that regard. The ordinary time limit for a law enforcement surveillance under Title III is 30 days, and extensions are strictly limited. For a FISA surveillance, the ordinary time limit is 90 days for foreign agents (one year in the case of a foreign government) and extensions are much more easily obtained. The PATRIOT Act raises FISA's 90-day limit to 120 days for foreign agents who are not U.S. citizens, and it doubles, from 45 to 90 days, the period during which foreign agents, including U.S. citizens, can be subjected to clandestine physical searches.[31] These lengthy periods of largely indiscriminate monitoring plainly would be impermissible in connection with an ordinary criminal investigation.

The significance of these expanded time limits is compounded by an important shift in the availability of FISA warrants in criminal investigations. Prior to September 11, the FISA regime was available only when "*the* purpose of the surveillance [or physical search] is to obtain foreign intelligence information."[32] If a FISA surveillance uncovered evidence warranting criminal prosecution, the evidence was admissible at the trial. But it nonetheless remained clear that the permissive FISA regime could be used only when foreign intelligence objectives were paramount.[33]

The PATRIOT Act alters this limitation by requiring only that "*a significant* purpose of the surveillance [or physical search] is to obtain foreign intelligence information."[34] This is a small change in statutory wording, but a large change in law enforcement power. Flexible FISA procedures permit searches and surveillance without probable cause to believe a crime is being committed, electronic surveillance can last for 90 days (three times the period allowed in investigating domestic crime), there is only minimal judicial control of particularity and the scope of surveillance, and clandestine physical searches (normally impermissible in investigating domestic crime) are allowed for 90-day periods with no showing of special need. FBI agents and prosecutors now can deploy these broad powers against both citizens and foreign nationals—even when their primary purpose is to investigate ordinary offenses and gather evidence for a criminal prosecution.

JUSTIFICATIONS FOR EXPANDED FISA POWERS. Even with its expanded post–September 11 reach, FISA surveillance is available only when there is reason to consider the target a foreign agent. For many Americans, this proviso will suffice to justify surveillance with no holds barred, especially when it evokes the picture of an Iraqi spy, a military or political attaché at the Russian Embassy, or an al Qaeda operative like Mohammed Atta. But this picture and the justification it seems to support are misleading in two respects.

Foreign agents usually do not announce their roles publicly. FISA surveillance therefore is typically predicated only on the unconfirmed *possibility* that the person targeted is a foreign agent. American citizens and foreign nationals who in fact have no connection to hostile foreign powers can be searched and subjected to broad FISA surveillance when there is a reasonable (although mistaken) suspicion of a foreign connection. Perhaps paradoxically, the broad surveillance allowed under FISA is considered unconstitutional when it is supported only by probable cause to believe that the person targeted is a mass murderer or a serial rapist. If that Fourth Amendment judgment is correct, there are reasons to be cautious about broad surveillance that rests on the much weaker foundation of probable cause to believe that the person targeted may be linked in some way to a foreign power.

FISA's broad conception of who qualifies as a foreign agent compounds this concern. The statute does not require actual or even suspected ties to a terrorist group or a hostile foreign government, and it does not require that the person targeted be suspected of any illicit activity whatever. A foreign power under FISA includes any "foreign-based political organization not substantially composed of United States persons," and a foreign agent includes any foreign national employed by such an organization.[35] Thus, a non-American spokesperson or fund-raiser for the British Labour Party or for a German environmental activist group is considered a foreign agent and while in the United States can be targeted for several months of eavesdropping, wiretapping, and clandestine physical searches to gain "foreign intelligence information," a term defined so broadly that it includes any "information . . . that relates to . . . the conduct of the foreign affairs of the United States."[36] U.S. citizens having (or reasonably believed to have) links to such organizations can be considered foreign agents and targeted for similar FISA surveillance under certain circumstances as well.[37]

The innovation introduced by the PATRIOT Act is to expose these U.S. citizens and foreign nationals to broad FISA surveillance when the government's primary purpose is *not* to gather foreign intelligence but instead to gather evidence for use at a criminal trial.

This is a momentous expansion of government power to conduct wide-ranging surveillance and secret physical searches. Yet the change seeks to address a genuine and extremely difficult problem. September 11 made tragically clear that the traditional division between law enforcement and foreign intelligence operations, always somewhat artificial, had lost virtually all meaning in the context of large-scale international terrorist groups such as al Qaeda.

That development puts two vital, deeply grounded principles of American government on a collision course. On the one hand, the president has an unquestioned responsibility to protect the nation against foreign attack and to prevent hostile foreign powers from conducting covert intelligence activity within our borders. On the other hand, law enforcement power, always potentially dangerous to a free society, may operate only within boundaries established by the Bill of Rights. And one of those boundaries, emphatically reaffirmed in the *Keith* case, is that law enforcement agents must submit to judicial scrutiny of the basis and scope of any surveillance that seeks evidence for criminal prosecutions—national security prosecutions included. Each of these principles seems applicable and each can easily swallow the other in a world where foreign threats emanate from terrorist groups that combine the worst features of a clandestine conspiracy with the most dangerous powers (and none of the restraining responsibilities) of a foreign state.

PRESERVING FISA AND THE FOURTH AMENDMENT. There are several possible ways to negotiate the foreign intelligence dilemma. One seemingly simple solution would be to permit foreign intelligence gathered under FISA to be used for protective and preventive purposes but to forbid any use of FISA intelligence in criminal prosecutions. This is a plausible approach, but the line it draws is clearer in theory than in practice. An effective defense against terrorism requires all investigators to coordinate their efforts and share what they know. But as soon as they do that, it becomes difficult for prosecutors to demonstrate that they had no help from leads generated by off-limits FISA intelligence. If taken seriously, the rule would force law enforcement investigators to steer clear of FISA material whenever they were intent on building a winnable case. And if FISA intelligence enabled investigators to preempt a terrorist attack and arrest those involved, the rule could make it impossible to put those apprehended on trial. These problems almost certainly foreclose the solution of granting broad authority for FISA surveillance while prohibiting use of its results in criminal trials.*

A second approach could focus not on how the surveillance is used but rather on the status of the person who is its target.[38] When a known foreign agent (the ambassador of a foreign government, for example) is targeted, it seems plausible to think that ordinary Fourth Amendment protections should not apply, perhaps because of some mutually accepted notion of the "rules of the game." But it is much less plausible to suggest that foreign nationals and American citizens lose ordinary Fourth Amendment protection merely because there is probable cause to believe (perhaps incorrectly) that they are linked to a foreign organization. Even when a person is suspected of murder, he has a Fourth Amendment right to judicial control of the basis and scope of a search for evidence against him; surveillance of a person reasonably believed to be a professional hit man must conform to the restrictions of Title III. It is hard to see why a citizen or lawful resident should be entitled to less protection merely because he is believed to be performing acts (including legal acts) for a foreign power.

It therefore seems that the controlling justification for relaxed standards in foreign intelligence surveillance is its distinctive *purpose*. In many other contexts, the Supreme Court has permitted searches under flexible standards, when they serve "special needs, beyond the normal need for law enforcement."[39] Protective and preventive goals in areas affecting public safety have provided the basis for the Court's approval of blood testing to detect illicit drugs and highway roadblocks to identify drunk drivers and get off them off the roads.[40] But the Court has held that essentially identical blood tests and roadblocks must satisfy traditional Fourth Amendment requirements when protective and preventive objectives become secondary to a predominant law enforcement purpose.[41] In accord with this view, one federal court ruled explicitly, during the Vietnam era, that foreign intelligence surveillance requires a traditional Fourth Amendment warrant when law enforcement purposes become paramount.[42] Unless the Court is moved to abandon this approach in the wake of September

---

*Compounding this problem, the Supreme Court consistently has viewed the exclusion of evidence at criminal trials as a remedy for an *illegal* search. Congress, of course, can mandate broader remedies. But if the intrusion itself is permissible (as it would be if it were properly authorized under FISA), then support for a rule barring prosecutors from using its fruits will be difficult to garner.

11, FISA surveillance under relaxed standards inevitably will be held unconstitutional when its primary purpose is to gather evidence for use in criminal prosecution.

As in several other areas of increased government power since September 11, the FISA amendments are both overbroad and dangerously shortsighted. It is surely difficult—and imprudent—to attempt a sharp separation of law enforcement and intelligence functions in a terrorism investigation. But that problem provides no justification for open-ended FISA surveillance and clandestine searches intended primarily to gather evidence for a conventional theft, fraud, or income-tax prosecution. At the same time, FISA's constitutional flaws will jeopardize convictions affected by the new regime, even in cases that involve the gravest terrorism charges.

The newly added FISA powers and their bypass of significant judicial control are justifiable only in the small subset of cases that involve an international terrorist element. And even in those cases, investigative needs are adequately served by limiting FISA to surveillance in which intelligence gathering is the primary (though not necessarily the sole) purpose. When criminal prosecution has become the primary goal, traditional Fourth Amendment restrictions on the executive branch remain important and, in all likelihood, constitutionally required safeguards.

Chapter 6

ENLARGING ACCESS TO FINANCIAL, EDUCATIONAL, AND BUSINESS RECORDS

In a series of decisions in the 1970s, the Supreme Court ruled that the Fourth Amendment does not protect the privacy of information voluntarily provided to third parties, such as the records of a person's checking transactions held by her bank.[1] Congress recognized that these rulings created a gap in the system of appropriate safeguards for personal privacy,[2] and it subsequently enacted statutes to limit government access to financial records, student records held by schools and colleges, and several other sorts of personal information.[3] These statutes do not provide the full complement of Fourth Amendment protections, but they offer other significant safeguards. Under the Right to Financial Privacy Act (RFPA), for example, banks are required, before complying with a government subpoena, to give notice to the customer, and customers who object have the right to a judicial hearing at which a court must decide whether the records are relevant to a legitimate governmental inquiry.[4]

In foreign intelligence investigations, the government was allowed more leeway, even before September 11. The FBI was allowed access to a person's bank records without giving her notice or an opportunity to contest the demand; in fact, the bank was barred from revealing that a foreign intelligence disclosure had been made, and the FBI did not need a court order—a letter request to the bank was sufficient.

But to obtain such access, an FBI official was required to certify that the records were sought for a foreign intelligence purpose and that there were specific facts showing that the customer was the agent of foreign power.[5] Similarly, FISA authorized the FBI to obtain, again on a surreptitious basis, the records of a limited class of travel-related businesses (buses, airplanes, and railroads; physical storage facilities; car rental companies; and hotels and motels—but not restaurants). But access to these records, like access to financial records, required the FBI to certify its foreign intelligence purpose and attest that there were specific facts confirming that the customer implicated was a foreign agent.[6]

DEVELOPMENTS SINCE SEPTEMBER 11

GOVERNMENT POWERS TO DEMAND PREVIOUSLY PRIVATE DOCUMENTS AND RECORDS

The PATRIOT Act loosens the pre–September 11 safeguards in significant and cumulatively far-reaching ways. To access financial records, FBI officials no longer need to certify that they have reason to consider the targeted customer a foreign agent; it is sufficient that the inquiry has any foreign intelligence or counterterrorism purpose.[7] A parallel change opens up access to telephone billing records on the same diluted basis.[8] The act amends a major federal statute governing the privacy of educational records to suspend all state and federal confidentiality protections and permit Justice Department access to student records, whenever a federal official certifies that the records are "likely to contain information . . . relevant to an authorized investigation . . . of domestic or international terrorism," again without any need to claim that the person targeted is a foreign agent or a suspect in the investigation.[9]

The FISA provisions granting access to the records of travel-related businesses (principally buses, trains, airlines, car rental companies, hotels, and motels) come in for significant change as well. The PATRIOT Act expands those provisions to permit FBI access to the books, documents, and records of *any* business (and apparently any non-business entity as well).[10] As written, the new provision applies to employee and patient records as well as customer records; it applies to such businesses as credit-card companies,

HMOs, magazine publishers, book sellers, and video rental stores; and it apparently reaches the files of such non-commercial entities as the Arab-American Anti-Defamation League, the Sierra Club, or any synagogue or mosque.[11] And these amendments (like the amendments for financial records) drop the previous requirement that the records had to be those of a suspected foreign agent. Records pertaining to any American citizen now are available for FBI inspection on a clandestine basis whenever the agent states that the records "are sought for an authorized investigation . . . to protect against international terrorism," whether or not there is a basis for considering the targeted person a suspect or a foreign agent.

The only mildly reassuring limit on the new powers is a proviso, repeated in several of the amendments, that demands for access to these records cannot be grounded on "an investigation of a United States person . . . conducted *solely* on the basis of activities protected by the first amendment."[12] But this limit affords little comfort since no agent would admit to launching an investigation on the basis of nothing more than a cleric's radical speech. Presumably, an agent's decision to go forward would be premised on suspicion or fear that the speaker intended to aid or encourage acts of violence, and at that point the investigation no longer would be based solely on protected activity. Even with a concern about possible violence in the background, however, such an investigation could be unconscionably intrusive. Demands for access to a list of a mosque's members, for example, or an Islamic charity's contributors violate long-settled constitutional protections for freedom of association.[13] Even if FBI actions of that sort prove to be rare (and, of course, there is no guarantee that they will be), they will chill religious freedom and have powerfully corrosive effects on democratic debate and political dissent.

On a more mundane level, personal matters once considered private and confidential—banking statements, courses taken in college, video rentals, and bookstore purchases—are now fair game for curious FBI and Treasury agents following hunches about where evidence of terrorism may lurk. And those exposed to this sort of snooping will be not only those who have something to hide. As the new rules make entirely clear, they are not—and were not intended to be—limited to records that pertain to agents of foreign terrorist groups or individuals who are in some way suspected of wrongdoing. It is enough that the investigating agent thinks there is a valuable lead to be found in the records of a perfectly law-abiding citizen.

OBLIGATORY SURVEILLANCE BY PRIVATE CITIZENS

The PATRIOT Act also expands the obligations imposed on private parties to report on the activities of others—in effect to be conscripted as eyes and ears for the government. Since 1970, federal statutes aimed at preventing money laundering have imposed important reporting requirements on banks and other financial institutions. In particular, financial institutions are required to file with the Treasury a Currency Transaction Report (CTR) for any cash transaction of more than $10,000.[14] And since 1992, they have been required to file a Suspicious Activity Report (SAR) whenever a customer's transactions seem illegal or simply unusual—for example, when the institution "has reason to suspect" that the transaction is "not the sort [of transaction] in which the particular customer would normally be expected to engage."[15] Financial institutions have been told that activities that can trigger a duty to report (and heavy fines if the institution fails to do so) include cases in which a customer "has an unusual concern for secrecy," is reluctant to provide information about the party for whom he acts, or "has a questionable background, including prior criminal convictions."[16]

For the year 2000, the Treasury received more than twelve million CTRs and 162,000 SARs, and the volume of these filings was increasing steadily. By spring 2001, the Treasury was receiving more than 15,000 SARs per month.[17]

The PATRIOT Act acknowledges that even before September 11, the volume of these reports was "interfering with effective law enforcement,"[18] and it requires the Secretary of the Treasury to study ways to *reduce* the number of submissions.[19] But in the meantime, the act takes large steps in the opposite direction. The obligation to file SARs is now imposed not only on financial institutions but also on all securities brokers and dealers.[20] The obligation to file a CTR for any cash transaction over $10,000 has been extended from financial institutions to "[a]ny person . . . who is engaged in a trade or business."[21] Treasury Regulations announced in April implement these obligations for credit-card companies, Western Union, check-cashing and currency-exchange businesses, and securities brokers and dealers; implementing regulations for insurance companies, travel agents, and automobile dealers are expected soon.[22] And the activities that require the filling of an SAR extend far beyond the realm of terrorism, organized crime, and big-time money laundering; securities brokers and dealers must now file an SAR for "any suspicious transaction relevant to a possible violation of law *or regulation.*"[23]

To further enhance Treasury's ability to spot "suspicious activity," the act suspends normal bank secrecy rules (state and federal) so that financial institutions now may share information *with one another* regarding individuals suspected of possible terrorist or money laundering activity—without facing any liability to their customers for doing so.[24] This step will make more banks aware of more reasons for considering customer transactions suspicious and will further increase the flow of reports to the government, which may or may not help combat terrorism. Either way, the implications of this change for a customer's ability to maintain confidentiality vis-à-vis competitors and *private sector* snoops are far-reaching and as yet barely understood.

The new focus on terrorism, moreover, dramatically extends the practical effect of these provisions. Drug dealers, the principal target of money-laundering enforcement before September 11, must transfer and sanitize literally billions of dollars of "dirty" money each year, so a relatively limited group of transactions will involve aggregate dollar amounts large enough to warrant attention. Lethal terrorist activity, unfortunately, is all-too-cheap; any net capable of picking up transactions to support it will need to be extraordinarily far-reaching and free of loopholes. The government estimates, for example, that the September 11 attacks cost a total of only $500,000 transferred over many months from oil-producing sites such as the United Arab Emirates, from which a large volume of high-dollar legitimate transactions also emanate.[25] Using wire transfers rather than cash and as many as thirty-five separate accounts, the hijackers managed to evade the reporting requirements then in place, and many of their transfers would not have been picked up even by the elaborate new system that now requires reports on tens or hundreds of thousands of additional transactions annually.[26]

COSTS AND BENEFITS

We can hope that Treasury and FBI analysts will rise to these challenges. The government's view is that it is "worth the effort to try to root out any possible leads."[27] But there has been little effort to assess the actual likelihood of finding these microscopic clues or to compare it to the administrative costs imposed on the private sector and to the privacy of personal transactions sacrificed in the process. The Treasury estimates that the preparation of an SAR, including the internal review of records to determine whether an activity requires reporting, should take an average of only three hours per form;[28] the Securities Industry Association believes, however, that "because of the difficulty of analyzing very complex transactions, in most cases the process of determining whether an activity requires reporting will take much more time, and in some cases can take several days, and at times weeks."[29]

The impact on individuals is of course more important but impossible to quantify. For many years prior to September 11, bankers were "under constant pressure to protect customers' privacy."[30] But when the PATRIOT Act was under consideration, both financial industry lobbyists and consumer privacy groups, reluctant to appear opposed to the war on terrorism, remained largely silent about the issues.[31]

Are these far-reaching sacrifices of personal privacy really necessary? And will they really aid investigations more often than they will flood them with "noise"? With all due concern to resist apocalyptic visions of the future, it is hard to suppress the fear that these sweeping new tools of investigation open the door to an extraordinarily powerful federal police presence in American lives. It is hard to resist the suspicion that there are better, more discriminating ways to proceed, without in any way hampering smart, effective foreign intelligence and counterterrorism efforts.

Chapter 7

REDUCING SUPERVISION OF
FIELD INVESTIGATORS

Since September 11, we have made more powerful surveillance tools available to frontline investigators and decreased their need for independent judicial approvals. We also have decreased *internal* supervision and control by senior officials in the FBI field offices and at headquarters in Washington. On May 30, 2002, Attorney General Ashcroft removed long-standing limits on the discretion of local agents to open files, conduct surveillance, and collect intelligence information. Behind these steps, of course, is not only the general assumption that more surveillance might have prevented the events of September 11 but also the specific news that in July and August, FBI agents in Phoenix and Minneapolis had pressed for an investigation of flight training by Middle Eastern men linked to al Qaeda, only to be rebuffed by overly cautious supervisors in Washington.

At his press conference announcing the new guidelines, Attorney General Ashcroft described a seemingly absurd set of obstacles posed by prior FBI standards, which discouraged agents from exploring hunches and drawing on routine sources of information that ordinary citizens use freely every day, for example, by surfing the web or attending meetings open to any member of the public. He explained that shortly after September 11, he had authorized the FBI to waive those restrictions when necessary in terrorism-related cases, but he said he was "disappointed that [this authority] was not used more widely." As a result, he concluded, "greater authority to investigate more vigorously needs to be given directly to FBI field agents."[1]

The new regulations allow FBI agents to consult sources open to anyone and to hire commercial "data mining" firms to collect publicly available information from the Internet. They eliminate administrative approvals that had been required prior to investigating political and religious groups, and now subject these organizations to scrutiny under the same terms applicable to the investigation of any other entity. Also eliminated were rules that barred use, at the early "preliminary inquiry" stage, of certain intrusive investigative techniques, such as interviews with a potential suspect's employer and coworkers, and mail covers (screening his mail by recording information on the envelope). Limits on the use of other intrusive investigative techniques during a preliminary inquiry were relaxed, as were the limits on how long preliminary inquiries can be continued when initial efforts uncover no evidence of criminal activity. And decision-making in all these matters was decentralized, with much greater control left to the fifty-six local FBI field offices.

THE FBI'S ROLE

It would be unfair to dismiss these moves to "unleash" the FBI as merely an overreaction to September 11. Some additional flexibility in investigative standards is appropriate if the decision to alter the FBI's mission is sound in the first place. For nearly all of its history, the bureau focused its attention on solving crimes already committed and acquiring admissible evidence sufficient to prove the offense in court. Though the bureau has long had agents assigned to counterespionage, and more recently counterterrorism, these analytic and preventive functions were marginal (even more so as the cold war waned) in an organization where the principal marks of success were making arrests and winning convictions.

The nation clearly needs a federal agency charged with an aggressively proactive counterterrorism mission. But it is not clear that this agency should be the FBI. With its distinctive culture, recruiting traditions, and training procedures, the FBI would have to reinvent itself thoroughly to make counterterrorism its principal priority and to carry out that mission successfully. To expect a large, tradition-bound bureaucracy to quickly reorient its operations and change its fundamental culture is about as realistic as expecting the world's largest ocean liner to stop itself instantly and turn around on a dime. It might therefore make more sense to preserve the FBI as a primarily reactive, crime-solving agency and to build a new organization, perhaps a domestic equivalent of the CIA, to take charge of counterterrorism efforts.

The stakes are high: our success in preventing terrorist attacks and the civil liberties impact of lodging broad intelligence-gathering power in a traditional law enforcement agency. Yet there is no indication that the administration has given thought to these concerns or considered any alternative to putting this job in FBI hands. The decision to change radically the mission of a large federal agency is a momentous step that demands full exploration both within the administration and in consultation with Congress.

JUSTIFICATION FOR REDUCED SUPERVISION

Whatever agency eventually takes charge, counterterrorism efforts require a capacity to take initiative quickly. To that extent, some easing of supervisory control has a place in the new picture. But even with a full appreciation of this need, there are reasons for concern and puzzlement about the new guidelines. In explaining his decision to drop prior restrictions, the attorney general seemed to ignore or trivialize the extraordinary abuses that give rise to them. And he managed to pass entirely unnoticed the fact that he had expanded *only* the power of field agents to investigate ordinary crime and suspected terrorism of the purely domestic variety. The new powers have *nothing whatever* to do with blocking al Qaeda and the international terrorists that preoccupy the American public.

BAIT AND SWITCH

The old Justice Department rules were entitled "The Attorney General's Guidelines on General Crimes, Racketeering Enterprise and Domestic Security/Terrorism Investigations." The May 30 amendments drop the word "Domestic" from the title and add to the preamble a phrase stressing the need to protect the American people from "foreign aggressors."* Nevertheless, the new guidelines reaffirm that "investigations and information collection relating to international terrorism, foreign counterintelligence, or foreign intelligence" continue to be governed, as they were before September 11, by a separate set of classified—but undoubtedly more permissive—foreign intelligence guidelines.[2] As a result, the old guidelines that Attorney General Ashcroft criticized were no obstacle to uncovering the September 11 plot or preventing future acts of international terrorism. The guidelines that are relevant in that regard, the foreign intelligence guidelines, were not faulted, and the Justice Department has indicated no intention to change them.

The first step in assessing the newly conferred powers, therefore, is to be clear on the kinds of investigations for which they really are intended—ordinary federal crime of all sorts, racketeering, and terrorism of the purely homegrown variety, such as the Oklahoma City bombing. Of course, no one should minimize these problems, the last in particular. And some of the more troubling new powers (such as the authority to attend—and therefore monitor—the public events of political and religious groups) are available only in investigations with a counterterrorism dimension.

But other newly delegated powers can be used no matter how routine the suspected offense. Investigations of ordinary theft or misuse of federal property and suspected gambling, prostitution, or sale of pornography are included. Local agents acting on a mere hunch or rumor concerning such offenses can now pursue a "preliminary inquiry," even when it produces no objective factual confirmation, for 180 days—double the time previously allowed—and can get successive extensions for 90 days each—triple the time previously allowed. And in pursuing that inquiry, based only on a hunch or rumor, field agents can now use intrusive investigative techniques previously barred, such as interviewing the potential suspect's employer. Congress and the press might have asked many more questions about these measures, if the attorney general had made clear the kinds of investigations they will enlarge—those involving ordinary federal crime, but *not* those aimed at countering international terrorism.

---

*The revised document is now entitled "The Attorney General's Guidelines on General Crimes, Racketeering Enterprise and Terrorism Enterprise Investigations."

THE RISKS

At least where terrorism investigations are concerned, old limits on agents' investigative discretion certainly should be open to reconsideration. The potential gains from easing those limits are obvious. But are there significant dangers in dropping objective prerequisites for an investigation, relaxing time limits on how long it can be pursued, and conferring broad discretion on investigating agents in the field? The parts of the new guidelines that Attorney General Ashcroft spotlighted—those granting field agents the authority to read the newspaper, surf the Internet, or attend meetings open to any member of the public—sound innocuous enough. But the safeguards he dismantled have a history that remains pertinent, in fact especially pertinent, in the context of the aggressively proactive intelligence work he seeks to encourage.

DISCRETION IN OPERATION, 1950–1976. The pre–September guidelines, adopted during the administration of President Gerald Ford and carried forward with minor adjustments by every administration since, were a response to serious management failures and civil liberties abuses that came to light during the 1960s and 1970s. The FBI agents of that era were not constrained to investigate only credible allegations of past crime. Free to pursue random tips and their own hunches, they intimidated dissidents, damaged the reputations of many who were not, and produced thick dossiers on politicians, other public figures, political and religious groups, and literally hundreds of thousands of individuals. And FBI Director J. Edgar Hoover did not hesitate to use the bureau's extensive dossiers to enhance his power, silence opponents, and ensure the support of important members of Congress.

Today, many who are unaware of that history are inclined to dismiss claims about egregious FBI misconduct in the recent past as the hyperbolic complaints of the oversensitive and the radical fringe. Few recall that the gravity of those FBI abuses and their staggering extent were documented extensively in the 1976 report of a bipartisan congressional committee (the Church Committee), many of whose members had begun the inquiry confidently assuming that the charges against the FBI were simply false or wildly exaggerated. In this regard, remarks made to the Church Committee by Senator Phillip Hart are especially relevant now:

I have been told for years . . . that this [misconduct] is exactly what the Bureau was doing all of the time, and . . . I assured them that they were [wrong]—it just wasn't true. . . . I did not believe it. The trick now, Mr. Chairman, is for this committee to be able to figure out how to persuade the people of this country that indeed it did go on. And how shall we insure that it will never happen again? But *it will happen repeatedly unless we can bring ourselves to understand and accept that it did go on.*[3]

It is therefore essential to recall the results of actual experience with broad investigatory discretion similar to that just restored at the FBI. Agents zealously pursuing leads and hunches saw nothing wrong in showing their badge and "just asking" employers and teachers whether an individual had been seen with communists, had expressed hatred of America, or had shown a desire to commit violent acts against the government. Agents spent years infiltrating and monitoring political groups of all stripes, from the Socialist Workers Party on the left to the Conservative American Christian Action Council and the John Birch Society on the right. Attending rallies and meetings open to the public, they monitored and maintained extensive files on student groups on college campuses, civil rights organizations including the National Association for the Advancement of Colored People (NAACP) and the Southern Christian Leadership Conference, national leaders such as the Rev. Martin Luther King, Jr., anti-war groups, and meetings they identified with the "Women's Liberation Movement."[4]

Investigations of the NAACP, initiated on suspicion that the group had ties to communists, continued for years even though agents reported that the NAACP strenuously avoided such ties. Anti-war and civil rights groups were monitored on the pretext (not always unfounded) that these groups might plan illegal marches, sit-ins, or trespass demonstrations at civilian or military facilities. Martin Luther King, Jr., was subjected to years of surveillance, legal and illegal, to determine whether his professed commitment to nonviolence was a sham and to acquire personal information that could be used to discredit him.

The Church Committee found, moreover, that "[i]ntelligence activities [tend] to expand beyond their initial scope . . . . Intelligence collection programs naturally generate ever-increasing demands for new data. . . . [Investigations have] swept in vast amounts of information about the personal lives, views, and associations of American citizens."[5] One agent who supported the effort to collect such intelligence nonetheless acknowledged that some investigators "would construe political considerations to be national security considerations, [and] move from the kid with a bomb to the kid with a picket sign, and from [there] to the kid with the bumper sticker of the opposing candidate. And you just keep going down the line."[6] By 1975, FBI headquarters held over half a million domestic intelligence files, most containing information on more than one individual, and there were many additional files in the field offices. In 1972 alone, the bureau opened 65,000 new domestic intelligence files.[7]

In the name of anticipating disorder, protecting national security, and unearthing hidden links to a radical extremist movement (communism), FBI agents, sometimes with direction from Washington and often on their own initiative, had damaged reputations, disrupted legitimate protest groups, and "deter[red] the exercise of First Amend[ment] rights."[8] The bureau was quite simply out of control.

NEEDS AND DANGERS IN 2002. The challenge that now faces the Justice Department is to create a framework for vigorous intelligence gathering and rapid initiatives in counterterrorism matters, without opening the door to the abuses of the past or their contemporary equivalents. As Justice Powell wrote for the Court in the *Keith* case, "[n]ational security cases . . . often reflect a convergence of First and Fourth Amendment values not present in cases of 'ordinary crime.' Though the investigative duty of the executive may be stronger in such cases, so also is there greater jeopardy to constitutionally protected speech."[9] One need not fear the reappointment of a J. Edgar Hoover to worry that unbridled discretion to build files, ask embarrassing questions, and spy on dissident political and religious minorities could harm innocent individuals, stifle First Amendment freedoms, and waste limited investigative resources that now, more than ever, need to stay targeted on the most serious potential threats.

Nor can we be confident that today's field offices and individual agents can be counted on to act wisely and selectively without central supervision. Even after complying with the more stringent pre-2002 guidelines, an FBI field office recently won national ridicule by spending six months, much of it after September 11, wiretapping a well-known New Orleans brothel to investigate the scope of prostitution in that city.[10]

In this regard, the Church Committee's findings on the subject of "accountability and control" have particular contemporary relevance:

The overwhelming number of excesses continuing over a prolonged period of time were due in large measure to the fact that the
system of checks and balances . . . was seldom applied to the intelligence community. Guidance and regulation . . . has been vague.
. . . Presidents and other senior Executive officials, particularly
the Attorneys General, have virtually abdicated their constitutional responsibility to oversee and set standards for intelligence
activity.[11]

Against the background of that finding, the attorney general's
professed "disappoint[ment]" that field offices and agents had not
accepted his invitation to forego headquarters approvals, and his
determination to give them freer rein, reflects a jarring inattention
to historical experience and bipartisan congressional consensus. And
the new guidelines themselves, enhancing local discretion to pursue
inquiries into routine crime, reducing required thresholds of suspicion,
and lifting necessary administrative approvals across the board, seem
dangerously simpleminded. What is needed is greater flexibility—but
only in terrorism investigations—and good substitutes for safeguards
that are removed, not an effort to pretend that accountability can be
diluted with no risk, even in routine matters.

The Justice Department's new approach to the investigation of
political and religious groups is a particularly disturbing example.
The department explains that henceforth investigations that touch
political and religious organizations "will proceed according to the
principle of neutrality." Such organizations "will [not] be singled out
for special scrutiny," but neither will they get special protection;
agents will be free to "use the same investigative techniques they
would use when investigating any other type of organization."[12] And
since the new guidelines greatly relax the limits on using sensitive
investigative techniques (which the PATRIOT Act in turn makes more
readily available), the practical effect is to expose religious and political organizations to extensive monitoring without objective grounds
for suspicion and with little supervisory control.

This notion of placing political and religious entities on the same
plane as any other organization, as if their only legitimate claim were
a claim to equal treatment, reveals an indifference to constitutional
values that words cannot tactfully describe. The Justice Department's
approach suggests a complete lack of familiarity with the lessons of
FBI history in the 1960s, not to mention decades of Supreme Court

precedent mandating special solicitude for political association and speech.[13] Taken literally, the Justice Department's "neutrality" principle suggests unawareness that the Constitution contains a First Amendment.

A more technical but equally serious problem is posed by the decision to reduce oversight from headquarters and give vastly greater discretion to the field offices. At a time when the news is filled with expressions of admiration for the astute agents in Phoenix and Minneapolis and with frustration over tragic actions at headquarters that tied their hands, the decision to decentralize is easily understandable. Nonetheless, it remains unclear why the attorney general attributes this FBI failure to the abstract principle of central supervision rather than to the poor training or ineptitude of particular supervisors. As a bureaucratic defense mechanism, the decision to blame the organization chart is predictable, but the preference for decentralization in these circumstances amounts to little more than policy-making by anecdote. It proceeds as if we had never experienced the 1960s and the enormous waste and abuse that occurred when field offices and individual agents had the kind of discretion the attorney general has just returned to them. What the FBI field offices in all likelihood need is *better* supervision, not less of it. And this is not only an organizational matter but an issue with large civil liberties implications.

Chapter 8

NEXT STEPS

Three recurring problems mar the federal response to September 11—bad compromises, September 11 opportunism, and unchecked executive branch power that defeats traditional checks and balances.

- *Bad compromises.* Valuable liberties have been eroded with little or no prospect of a useful law enforcement payoff. Examples include new authority to monitor attorney–client communication; unnecessarily broad access to financial, educational, and business records; overbroad reporting obligations imposed on banks and businesses; and reduced supervision of investigating agents by their FBI superiors.

- *September 11 opportunism.* Investigative powers largely or totally unrelated to terrorism have slipped into the counterterrorism package and won approval without the scrutiny that proposals tied to a conventional law enforcement goal normally would face. Examples include new authority to investigate routine criminal cases by monitoring e-mail and Internet activity without probable cause, searching private premises secretly without notice to the owner, and using broad foreign intelligence powers even when there is no substantial counterterrorism or foreign intelligence purpose. Similarly, FBI field agents have gained enhanced power to conduct surveillance without supervisory approval or control in routine cases unrelated to terrorism.

- *Unchecked executive power.* Across the entire spectrum of federal responses to September 11, accountability safeguards are repeatedly, unnecessarily, and dangerously eroded; in some instances, traditional checks and balances have been obliterated entirely. Examples include indefinite detention of Americans and foreign nationals without judicial approval; imposition of secrecy concerning detention hearings and detainee identity, both without judicial approval; incommunicado detention that completely prohibits attorney–client communication, access to civilian courts, and all other contact with the outside world—even for an American citizen arrested within the United States; and new power to conduct many types of intrusive surveillance with little or no judicial oversight.

To a degree not yet widely appreciated, the federal executive branch, in the name of fighting a war on terrorism, has acquired comprehensive new powers to detain without charge, to restrict public hearings and access to counsel, to conduct secret searches, to spy electronically, and to obtain access to previously confidential financial, business, and educational files. To an extent that has received virtually no attention, many of these new powers *are not* limited to terrorism cases and *do not* require suspicion of any kind that the person targeted by the probe is involved in criminal activity. And often these new powers can be exercised *unilaterally*, without the supervisory control and judicial oversight that was taken for granted until September 11.

We can and must do better.

Our first priority must remain a vigorous, proactive effort to detect and avert new attacks. But that effort is often undermined by indiscriminate attempts simply to compile more and more information for its own sake, as if we had repealed the law of diminishing returns. We need to restore mechanisms that ensure greater focus and selectivity on the front end of the intelligence-gathering enterprise.

Beyond that, ten steps deserve urgent attention:

- Undertake a comprehensive, independent assessment of the causes of the intelligence failures leading up to September 11 and of the additional surveillance powers, if any, that would enable us to prevent comparable attacks in the future.

+ Reconsider the possibility of lodging responsibility for gathering and analyzing counterterrorism intelligence in an agency other than the FBI.

+ Repeal, pending separate study and enactment, the new surveillance and law enforcement powers not related to domestic or international terrorism.

+ Eliminate secret detention and secret hearings for American citizens and foreign nationals arrested within the United States, except when judicially approved for national security reasons demonstrated in a particular case.

+ Require prompt review by INS immigration judges for all detention of foreign nationals arrested within the United States, with access to the courts in cases of prolonged or indefinite detention; require judicial review, if necessary by the Foreign Intelligence Court or a comparable panel of Article III judges, for all pretrial detention of American citizens arrested within the United States.

+ Eliminate restrictions on communication with counsel by American citizens and foreign nationals arrested within the United States, except when judicially approved for public-safety or national security reasons demonstrated in a particular case.

+ Limit clandestine searches and surveillance under relaxed FISA standards to investigations in which the primary purpose is to gather foreign intelligence.

+ Review and narrow new powers to access financial, educational, and business records, especially those pertaining to individuals not considered to be foreign agents or terrorist suspects.

+ Review and narrow private-sector obligations to file currency-transaction and suspicious-activity reports.

+ Reinstate central-headquarters supervision of field investigators; tighten internal control over intrusive investigative techniques and over routine, nonterrorism investigations; provide flexibility, rapid analysis, and rapid response capabilities for central-headquarters supervisors in terrorism investigations.

September 11 was an extraordinary crisis, warranting emergency measures of extraordinary scope. But there is, unfortunately, no reason to believe that the threat of terrorism will recede any time soon. More likely, the "emergency" will be with us through several future presidential administrations. Thus, the enhanced size and prerogatives of the federal law enforcement establishment may not be reversed in our lifetimes. Along with concern for our safety and security, we must devote our utmost attention to the powers of the government under which we will live over that very long term.

NOTES

CHAPTER 1

1. U.S. Department of Justice, "FY 2003 Budget Request Highlights," available at www.usdoj.gov/jmd/2000-budget/fy2003.htm.

2. *Uniting and Strengthening America by Providing Appropriate Tools Required to Intercept and Obstruct Terrorism Act of 2001*, P.L. 107-56 (2001) (officially the USA PATRIOT Act, hereafter cited as PATRIOT Act).

CHAPTER 2

1. William H. Rehnquist, *All the Laws but One: Civil Liberties in Wartime* (New York: Alfred A. Knopf, 1998), p. 218.

2. See id., at 191.

3. See id., at 60.

4. Id., at 221.

5. *Ex parte Milligan*, 71 U.S. 2 (1866).

6. Id., at 122.

7. Id., at 127.

8. Id., at 109, 118.

9. "It can serve no useful purpose to inquire what those laws and usages are . . . . [N]o usage of war could sanction a military trial [where the courts are open and their processes unobstructed] for any offense whatever of a citizen in civil life, in nowise connected with the military service." Id., at 122.

10. "It is not easy to see how Milligan can be treated as a prisoner of war when he lived in Indiana for the past twenty years. . . . If in Indiana he conspired with bad men to assist the enemy, he is punishable for it in the Courts of Indiana."

11. Id., at 122, 127.

12. E.g., *Schenck v. United States*, 249 U.S. 47 (1919).

13. *United States v. Quirin*, 317 U.S. 1, 45–46 (1942).

69

14. *United States v. Hirabayashi,* 320 U.S. 81 (1943); *Korematsu v. United States,* 323 U.S. 214 (1944).

15. *Ex Parte Endo,* 323 U.S. (1944).

16. *Duncan v. Kahanamoku,* 327 U.S. 304 (1946); id. at 336 (Stone, C.J., concurring).

17. Id., at 343 (Burton, J., dissenting).

18. Id., at 322.

19. Id., at 336 (Stone, C.J., concurring) (quoting *Sterling v. Constantin,* 287 U.S. 378, 401).

20. *Youngstown Sheet & Tube Co. v. Sawyer,* 343 U.S. 579 (1952).

21. *United States v. United States District Court (Keith),* 407 U.S. 297 (1972).

22. *New York Times Co. v. United States,* 403 U.S. 713 (1971).

CHAPTER 3

1. Details released by the Justice Department in November 2001 and January 2002 are summarized, along with other available reports, in Amnesty International, "Concerns Regarding Post September 11 Detentions in the USA," AMR 51/044/2002 (hereafter cited as AI), at §3.4 (March 2002).

2. See *Gannett Co. v. DePasquale,* 443 U.S. 368 (1979); *Globe Newspaper Co. v. Superior Court,* 457 U.S. 596 (1982).

3. See AI §§4.2–4.4. The restrictions on access to detainees by attorneys, aid organizations, and family members all are contrary to normal INS policies. AI §§4.2–4.3.

4. See *American Civil Liberties Union of New Jersey v. County of Hudson,* 2002 WL 1285110 (N.J. Superior Court, June 12, 2002).

5. Attorney General John Ashcroft, press conference (November 27, 2001), available at www.usdoj.gov/ag/speeches/2001/agcrisisremarks11_27.htm.

6. See *Detroit Free Press v. Ashcroft,* 195 F. Supp. 937 (E.D. Mich, April 3, 2002).

7. Id.; Danny Hakim, "States Are Told to Keep Detainee Information Secret," *New York Times,* April 19, 2002, p. A14; *North Jersey Media Group, Inc. v. Ashcroft,* 2002 U.S. Dist. LEXIS 10136 (D.N.J., May 28, 2002).

8. *Zadvydas v. Davis,* 533 U.S. 678, 687–93 (2001).

9. See *United States v. Place,* 462 U.S. 696 (1983).

10. *County of Riverside v. McLaughlin,* 500 U.S. 44 (1991).

11. 18 U.S.C. §3142; *United States v. Salerno,* 481 U.S. 739 (1987).

12. 8 C.F.R. §287.3(d).

13. 8 C.F.R. §287.3(d) (September 17, 2001).

14. *PATRIOT Act* §412(a).

15. *County of Riverside v. McLaughlin,* 500 U.S. 44 (1991); *Gerstein v. Pugh,* 420 U.S. 103 (1975).

16. *Immigration and Nationality Act,* §236A(a)(5), as amended by *PATRIOT Act* §412(a).

17. AI §3.5.

18. AI §3.5.

19. AI §3.10.

20. See *Salerno,* 481 U.S. 739 , supra; *Zadvydas,* 533 U.S. 678, supra; *Foucha v. Louisiana,* 504 U.S. 71 (1992) (a dangerous individual cannot be detained indefinitely in the absence of a showing of mental illness or mental abnormality).

21. In 1942, eight German saboteurs who landed secretly in the United States were tried before a military commission and sentenced to death. The executive order establishing that commission provided for a secret proceeding for reasons specific to that case. See *Ex parte Quirin,* 317 U.S. 1 (1942). Apart from the fact that special military procedures apply to the trial of enemy combatants, the imposition of secrecy on an ad hoc basis, for national security reasons specific to a particular case, cannot be considered a precedent for the secrecy restrictions imposed across the board in the case of all the September 11 detainees.

22. Katherine Q. Seelye, "U.S. Argues War Detainee Shouldn't See a Lawyer," *New York Times,* June 1, 2002, p. A10.

23. *Hamdi v. Rumsfeld,* no. 02-6827, U.S. Court of Appeals (4th Cir., June 4, 2002).

24. Philip Shenon, "Appeals Court Keeps an American Detainee and His Lawyer Apart," *New York Times,* July 13, 2002, p. A8.

25. E.g., *Duncan v. Kahanamoku,* 327 U.S. 304 (1946).

26. See Benjamin Weiser, "U.S. Defends Military Custody of Suspect in 'Dirty Bomb' Case," *New York Times,* June 27, 2002, p. A26.

27. See footnote on text page 4 above.

28. 71 U.S. 2, 127 (1866).

29. 327 U.S. 304 (1946); id. at 336, (Stone, C. J., concurring).

30. See *Ex parte Quirin,* 317 U.S. 1, 8 (1942).

31. 317 U.S. 1 (1942).

32. 317 U.S. 1, 19–20 (emphasis added).

33. U.S. Constitution, art. III (3).

34. See discussion at pp. 8–10 above.

CHAPTER 4

1. 28 C.F.R. §501.3(d), 66 Fed. Reg. 55062, 55066 (October 31, 2001).

2. C.F.R. §501.3(a).

3. See 18 U.S.C. §2518(3); *United States v. Carneiro,* 861 F.2d 1171, 1179 (9th Cir., 1998).

4. Cf. *Weatherford v. Bursey*, 429 U.S. 545 (1977).

5. 66 Fed. Reg. 55062, 55064 (October 31, 2001).

6. Letter of American Bar Association President Robert E. Hirshon to U.S. Department of Justice, Bureau of Prisons, "ABA Comments on BOP-1116, AG Order No. 2529-2001" (December 28, 2001), available at www.abanet.org/poladv/letters/exec.

7. See *Illinois v. Gates*, 462 U.S. 213 (1983).

8. *McCray v. Illinois*, 386 U.S. 300 (1967).

9. *United States v. United States District Court (Keith)*, 407 U.S. 297, 320–21 (1972).

CHAPTER 5

1. *PATRIOT Act*, §206 (roving surveillance); §209 (stored voice mail); §211 (cable companies); §§216, 219 & 220 (nationwide warrants).

2. James Risen and David Johnston, " F.B.I. Report Found Agency Not Ready to Counter Terror," *New York Times*, June 1, 2001, p. A1.

3. Id.

4. David Johnston and Don Van Natta, Jr., "Wary of Risk, Slow to Adapt, F.B.I. Stumbles in Terror War," *New York Times*, June 2, 2002, pp. 1, 31.

5. U.S. Department of Justice, "FY 2003 Budget Request Highlights," available at www.usdoj.gov/jmd/2000-budget/fy2003.htm.

6. See *PATRIOT Act* §366.

7. FBI internal e-mail, dated 4/5/00, to Spike (Marion) Bowman, released to the Electronic Privacy Information Center on May 24, 2002, available at www.epic.org/privacy/carnivore/5_02_release.html.

8. U.S. Constitution, amend. IV.

9. 407 U.S. at 320.

10. Id., at 314.

11. *Katz v. United States*, 389 U.S. 347 (1967) (Harlan, J., concurring).

12. *United States v. White*, 401 U.S. 745 (1971).

13. *United States v. Miller*, 425 U.S. 435 (1976).

14. *Smith v. Maryland*, 442 U.S. 735 (1979); see *California v. Greenwood*, 486 U.S. 35 (1988).

15. U.S. Constitution, amend. IV.

16. *Berger v. New York*, 388 U.S. 41 (1967)

17. 18 U.S.C. §2501 et seq.

18. 18 U.S.C. §2511(3).

19. *United States v. United States District Court (Keith)*, 407 U.S. 297 (1972).

20. 50 U.S.C. §1801 et seq.

21. 50 U.S.C. §1804(a)(7)(B).

22. *United States v. Pelton*, 835 F.2d 1067, 1075 (4th Cir. 1987).

23. 18 U.S.C. §3123(a).

24. *PATRIOT Act* §216(c)(3).

25. "IIT Research Institute, Independent Review of the Carnivore System," Final Report (December 8, 2000) (hereafter cited as IITRI Report).

26. FBI internal e-mail, supra note 7.

27. IITRI Report, p. xiii.

28. *Richards v. Wisconsin*, 520 U.S. 385 (1997).

29. *PATRIOT Act*, §213.

30. 50 U.S.C. §§1823–1824.

31. *PATRIOT Act* §207(a)(2). The caption of this section refers to "Surveillance of Non-United States Persons," but the language extending the period for physical searches amends a section of FISA that applies to American citizens as well.

32. 50 U.S.C. §§1804(a)(7)(B), P.L. 95-511, 92 Stat. 1788 (1978) (emphasis added).

33. Courts generally allowed use of FISA procedures even when foreign intelligence gathering was not the government's *sole* purpose, for example, when agents pursuing a foreign intelligence inquiry could anticipate from the outset the possibility of using the fruits of surveillance in a criminal trial. *United States v. Duggan*, 743 F.2d 59, 78 (2d Cir., 1984). Though this interpretation left an obvious opening for prosecutors to do an end run around strict Title III requirements, FISA surveillance remained legitimate only when foreign intelligence gathering was the agents' primary purpose.

34. 50 U.S.C. §1804(a)(7)(B), as amended by *PATRIOT Act* §218 (emphasis added)

35. 50 U.S.C. §§1801(a)(5), 1801(b)(1)(A).

36. 50 U.S.C. §§1801(e)(2)(B).

37. 50 U.S.C. §§1801(b)(2).

38. The *Keith* decision seems to attach importance to this factor. The defendant there had been charged with bombing a CIA office, a facility with obvious foreign intelligence functions. But the Court insisted that normal Fourth Amendment judicial safeguards apply because there was no evidence that a foreign power was implicated in the commission of the crime; the Court "express[ed] no opinion as to . . . the issues which may be involved with respect to the activities of foreign powers or their agents." 407 U.S., at 309, 321–22.

39. *Ferguson v. City of Charleston*, 532 U.S. 67, 74 n.7 (2001); *Griffin v. Wisconsin*, 483 U.S. 868, 873 (1987).

40. *Treasury Employees v. Von Raab*, 489 U.S. 656 (1989); *Michigan Dept. of State Police v. Sitz*, 496 U.S. 444 (1990).

41. *Ferguson v. City of Charleston,* 532 U.S. 67 (2001); *City of Indianapolis v. Edmond,* 531 U.S. 32 (2001). In *Edmond,* the Court noted, as a possible "exigenc[y]" exception to this principle, that "the Fourth Amendment would almost certainly permit an appropriately tailored roadblock set up to thwart an *imminent* terrorist attack." 531 U.S., at 44 (emphasis added). Whatever its scope, that exception presumably would not extend to the entire ongoing regime of FISA surveillance.

42. *United States v. Truong Dinh Hung,* 629 F.2d 908, 915 (4th Cir., 1980). ("[T]he executive should be excused from securing a [traditional] warrant only when the surveillance is conducted 'primarily' for foreign intelligence reasons. . . . [O]nce surveillance becomes primarily a criminal investigation, . . . individual privacy interests come to the fore and government foreign policy concerns recede. . . . We thus reject the government's assertion that, if surveillance is to any degree directed at gathering foreign intelligence, the executive may ignore the warrant requirement of the Fourth Amendment.")

CHAPTER 6

1. E.g., *United States v. Miller,* 425 U.S. 435 (1976); *Smith v. Maryland,* 442 U.S. 735 (1979).

2. *McDonough v. Widnall,* 891 F.Supp. 1439 (D. Colo., 1995) (*The Right to Financial Privacy Act* was passed by Congress "in order to . . . fill in a void left by the Supreme Court's holding in *United States v. Miller.*")

3. *Bank Secrecy Act,* 12 U.S.C. §1951 et seq.; *Right to Financial Privacy Act,* 12 U.S.C. §3401 et seq.; *General Education Provisions Act,* 20 U.S.C. §1232g.

4. 12 U.S.C. §3410(c).

5. 12 U.S.C. §3414(a)(5)(A) (1978, 1982, 1986).

6. 50 U.S.C. §1862(b)(2).

7. 12 U.S.C. §§3414(a)(1)(C); 3414(a)(5)(A) (2001).

8. 18 U.S.C. §2709(b) (2001), as amended by *PATRIOT Act* §505(a) (2001).

9. 20 U.S.C. §1232g(j) (1) & (2) (2001), as amended by *PATRIOT Act* §507 (2001).

10. 50 U.S.C. §1861(a)(1) (2001), as amended by *PATRIOT Act* §215 (2001).

11. As before September 11, the caption of this section states its subject as "certain business records," and a court might therefore interpret it as limited to commercial enterprises. But in fact the text of the provision, unlike its predecessor, is *not* limited to business records, and there is no indication that it was intended to be so limited. The new provision applies